Pioneer Pho

new! *12"x12" frame*
Pet Scrapbooks

DOGS
&
CATS!

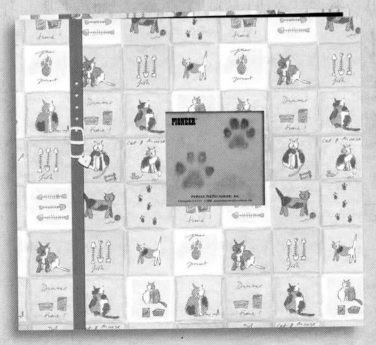

12" x 12" Top Loading Scrapbooks

Frame on the Front Cover
to Insert Your Favorite Pet Photo

Style No. MB-10PET

Pioneer Photo Albums, Inc.
(800) 366-3686 • (818) 882-2161 • Fax: 8188826239 • pioneer@pioneerphotoalbums.com

PIONEER

Katie Collection Shown

FRIPPERY
JEWELRY KITS

Editor

I must admit it. As much as I talk about photos being the most important things on a scrapbook page - and they are - I am completely in love with all the "extras." Sometimes I find myself opening up canisters, jars and bottles and rummaging through ribbon, buttons and brads for the sheer fun of seeing them. And don't get me started on flowers - I have to keep them in full view so I can enjoy them all the time, whether I'm attaching them to a page or just letting them brighten up my desk.

I recently taught a class about scrapbooking, and in an effort to impress the importance of journaling, I asked, "why scrapbook?" I was looking for the answer, "To preserve memories," but instead, the great answer I received was, "Because it's so much fun." And that is exactly right! Scrapbooking is all about photos and journaling and the recording of our fleeting and precious memories, but it is also all about the fun. This wonderful industry is full of companies who keep creating terrific products that make scrapbooking so enjoyable. Never before have there been so many great things to work with. This book is all about those fun embellishments and the joy of using them - so settle in, enjoy browsing, choose your favorites, then have *fun* using the inspiration gleaned to embellish your own great projects.

Pam

Publisher Chad Harvie

Editor in Chief Pam Baird

Assistant Editor Tammy Morrill

Contributing Editor/Designer Jeri Huish

Editorial Staff
Alisha Gordon, Kara Henry, Paige Taylor

Art Director Amy Noorda

Design & Photography Linda Nelson

Cover Photography Kaycee Leishman

Photography
Kristy Plessman, Mio Watanabe

Retail Sales
Jan Rudd
888-225-9199 x12
janr@scrapbooktrendsmag.com

Retail Sales Customer Service Sharee Johnson

Subscriptions/Customer Service
Sarah Dalsing, Skyler Rudd

Shipping/Receiving
Clinton Herndon, Tina Gonzales

Internet Customer Service
support@scrapbooktrendsmag.com

Advertising
Amber Hall
888-225-9199 x14
amberh@scrapbooktrendsmag.com

Advertising
Daren Phillipy
509-999-7908
darenphillipy@hotmail.com

Scrapbook Trends Magazine is published 12 times
a year by Northridge Media, LLC.
P.O. Box 1570 Orem, Utah 84059-1570
phone **888-225-9199** fax **801-225-6510**
e-mail: support@scrapbooktrendsmag.com
www.scrapbooktrendsmag.com

Subscriptions 1-888-225-9199
1 year U.S. subscription price: $24.97
2 year U.S. subscription price $44.97
3 year U.S. subscription price $62.97
1 year Canada/Mexico $40.97 (U.S. funds only)
Please call for other international rates.

Please send address changes to:
Northridge Media
P.O. Box 1570
Orem, Utah 84059-1570
or e-mail: support@scrapbooktrendsmag.com

Please send reader submissions to:
submissions@scrapbooktrendsmag.com,
submit@scrapbooktrendsmag.com, or
readers@scrapbooktrendsmag.com

Visit us online at:
scrapbooktrendsmag.com

Contents

features

sections

Like the flourish on the cover? This design
is available in stamp form, along with many
others, at greengrassstamps.com

Charms

---

charm

(chärm) *n.*

1. *the power or quality of pleasing or delighting; a delightful characteristic; a little ornament.*
2. *a small metal item added to a scrapbook page to increase its attractiveness.*

YOU'RE THE BEST!

Tammy Morrill

Card is 5" square
Cardstock and scalloped scissors: **Provo Craft** Paper and flower charm: **Making Memories**
Ribbon: **Lasting Impressions** Sentiment and photo corner stamps: **Green Grass Stamps** Ink:
StazOn

Scallop and sand one edge of a 5 x 1 1/4" block of striped paper; adhere it across your
card front. Use an edge distresser from Making Memories to add some texture to the
edges of your card, then add velvet ribbon, a flower charm and a tag. Stamp photo
corners for a finishing touch.

WARM UP

Courtney Kelly
of Colorado Springs, Colorado

Cardstock: **Bazzill Basics** Paper,
metal charms, ribbon: **American
Crafts** Font: **Timeless, from
fryfonts.com**

Let these metal charms from
American Crafts help inspire
your journaling – Courtney talks
about being warmed up on a cold
day by a kiss from her husband,
shown here in a winter photo.

Nothing warms you up quicker on that cold winter day than a special kiss from the one you love.

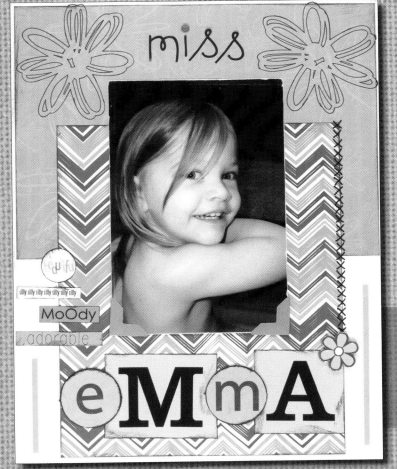

MISS EMMA

Amberley Stevens of London, Ontario, Canada

Cardstock: **Bazzill Basics** Paper: **Rob and Bob Studio,
Reminisce** Brad, flower charm, uppercase black letter
stickers: **Making Memories** Flower mask, photo corners,
pink decorative tape: **Heidi Swapp** Chipboard letter
circles: **Imagination Project** Lowercase black letter
stickers: **American Crafts** Word stickers: **KI Memories
and Doodlebug Design** Rub on stitches: **Die Cuts with
a View** Ink: Nick Bantock Pen: Zig

Amberley traced around a Heidi Swapp flower
mask at the top of her page and applied rub on
stitches down the right side of the zigzag paper
from Reminisce. A simple green metal flower from
Making Memories adds charm to this girly page.

KASSIDY

Alisha Gordon

Paper: **American Crafts** Charms: **Boxer Studios** Brads: **Making Memories** Chipboard letters: **Heidi Swapp** Pen: **Zig**

Divide your layout in half by stitching a 6 x 12" block of patterned paper over coordinating purple paper. Use flowers cut from the paper to embellish the photo and underneath the title. Accent the flowers with rhinestone brads and tie charms to your chipboard letters.

GO FISH

Debbie Hodge
of Durham, New Hampshire

Cardstock: **Bazzill Basics** Paper,
brads, charms, spiral clip: **American
Traditional Designs** Colored wire:
Making Memories Chipboard letters:
Heidi Swapp Pen: **Sakura**

String these fish charms from
American Traditional Designs
together with colored wire,
then fasten them in a vertical
row with brads. Add a single
fish off to the side for balance.

TOGETHER

Celeste Smith of West Hartford, Connecticut

Cardstock: **Die Cuts with a View** Paper: **American
Crafts, KI Memories, MOD** Metal "together" charm:
American Crafts Acrylic flower and token:
KI Memories Rub ons: **Autumn Leaves**

A simple charm can say it
all. The two figures in this
"together" charm echo the boys
in the photo. Colorful punched
squares of paper and creative
stitching complete the look.

Together - the dynamic between the two of you is incredible. One minute you are all smiles, craziness and
giggles; the next there are tears and wailing. Growing up my father always said to us, "you start out laughing
and you'll end up crying." I ticked me when he said this, but now I know exactly what he meant. I just hope that
you both will remember the smiles and giggles and forget the tears. For the love you have for each other truly
makes the tears irrelevant.

BABY

Paige Taylor

Card is 6 x 4"
Cardstock, chipboard, ink: **Bazzill Basics** Charms, stick pin: **Craft supply** Metal letters: **American Crafts** Acrylic letter: **Heidi Swapp** Stencil letter: **Chatterbox** Fabric: **Making Memories** Flowers: **SEI** Rub ons: **Memories Complete**

Fasten a pin to a swatch of fabric, threading on baby-themed charms as you go. Place it in the upper left-hand corner of your card and spell "baby" with an assortment of letters. Two crocheted flowers from SEI add to the soft feel of this baby card.

"If I were an **Opel**,"

I would take the most awesome photos • I would be a better daughter • I'd make one tasty Cosmopolitan • My friends would always receive the perfect present • I would hand cut all my titles • People would actually recognize me at church • I could assemble furniture without the help of a man • I could leave the house without a baseball cap to hide my matted hair • I would drive the cutest (and cleanest) car • Organization would be my middle name • The scrapbooking community would marvel at my pages • My purse and shoes would always match my outfit • I would have will power • I would travel more • I could have a snow day • My American flag would never collect dust in my shed • I would sing in public • I would actually know how to use my computer • I could easily recite the lyrics to any Pat Benatar song • I would be the best aunt a kid could have • I would know how to throw a fantastic party on a modest budget • I would be loved by people all across the U.S.A. • Well, an Opel I'm not; I'll just have to settle for being one of their lucky friends.

enjoy
life

OPEL

Gabriella Biancofiore
of Norridge, Illinois

Cardstock: **Archivers, Bazzill Basics**
Paper: **me & my BIG ideas** Word
charms: **Making Memories** Ribbon:
American Crafts Corner rounder: **Marvy**
Uchida Fonts: **Journaling Dingbats,**
twopeasinabucket.com, Libby Script,
momscorner4kids.com, Arial

Arrange your title in a word processing program, placing the words and quotes in moveable text boxes to get the placement just right. Journal below the title, separating each of your journaling items with colored bullets; print on the left side of a sheet of cardstock. Place a photo next to it and stack two word charms from Making Memories in the corner as a finishing touch.

HALLIE

Johanna Peterson
of El Cajon, California

Cardstock, vellum: **Bazzill**
Basics Mini eyelets:
Making Memories Charms:
Artchixstudio.com Jump
rings: **Westrim Crafts** Sea
glass: **Magic Scraps** Fibers:
Fiberartshop.com Stamps:
Hero Arts, PSX Ink: **StazOn**
Font: **Viner Hand ITC, from**
myfonts.com

Tie charms onto colorful fibers, then let those fibers run the length of the page. Johanna also stamped key words in her journaling on sea glass, then adhered the glass to printed vellum

God's greatest creation is not that he flung the stars or made the ocean waves, but the wonder of a child at each of them.

metal

met·al

(mĕt'l) *n.*

1. *any category of electropositive elements that usually have a shiny surface, can be melted or fused, hammered into thin sheets or drawn into wires.*
2. *metal objects can be shaped into photo corners, frames and tags, or used as word plaques that add an eye-catching touch to any paper crafting project.*

THANKS

Tina Gonzales

Card is 6" square
Cardstock: **Bazzill Basics** Paper: **MOD** Metal flowers: **Creative Imaginations** Ribbon: **Pebbles, Inc.** Die cut: **Cricut**

Pin two metal flower clips to a piece of cardstock with your sentiment. Adhere the piece to your card front and add a strip of ribbon across the top.

MOMENTS

Connie Petertonjes
of Liberty Township, Ohio

Cardstock, paper: **Wild Asparagus**
Grommets: **Dritz** Metal molding strip:
Making Memories Ribbon: **Close To
My Heart** Stamp: **Hero Arts** Ink: **Nick
Bantock** Pen: **Zig** Fonts: **AL Gettysburg
and AL Outdoors, both from the Autumn
Leaves Vintage Font CD** Quote: **From
"Quote Unquote" by Autumn Leaves**

Set three pairs of grommets, each
spaced about 1 1/4" apart; knot
sheer yellow ribbon through for a
dainty touch. Sand a metal strip
from Making Memories and adhere
it down the left side of your page.

WAITING

Brandy Brandon of Layton, Utah

Cardstock: **Bazzill Basics** Paper:
American Crafts Brads: **American
Crafts and unknown** Metal letters:
Making Memories Label holder: **7
Gypsies** Ribbon: **Offray, American Crafts**
Fonts: **Constitution, Roadtrip, both by
Creating Keepsakes**

Divide your layout in half by
adhering blocks of orange cardstock
and green dotted paper over a sheet
of black cardstock. Round the
corners of a large purple photo mat
and place it off-center. Balance the
page with two overlapping photos
and journaling strips. Knot ribbon
through metal eyelet letters and
adhere them under your main photo.

YOU'RE SWEET

Liana Suwandi of Wylie, Texas

Card is 4 x 5 1/2"
Cardstock, brad: **Bazzill Basics** Paper: **Melissa Frances** Metal word: **Provo Craft** Jewel: **Rob and Bob Studio** Flowers: **Prima** Ribbon: **SEI** Chipboard letters, rub ons: **Making Memories**
Photo corner: **Chatterbox** 3-D sticker: **Christina Cole** Sticker: **K & Company** Die cut: **Sizzix**

A photo corner doesn't have to go in the corner — set it on the end of an oval label holder for an unexpected twist. You can also try knotting a brown ribbon at the top of your card and zigzag stitching across both the ribbon and the knot.

MOM, I COLOR?

Jeri Huish

Cardstock: **Provo Craft** Paper and stickers: **American Crafts** Brads and word charms: **Making Memories** Font: **MA Flirty, from dafont.com**

Leave room for metal word charms as you type your journaling. Before printing, you may wish to allow for an inch or so of blank space on either end of the journaled lines. This way, if you're adding brads to the strips, you can play around with the arrangement before finalizing it and trimming off the end you don't need. You may want to right or left justify all the strips, or you may want to stagger them as Jeri did.

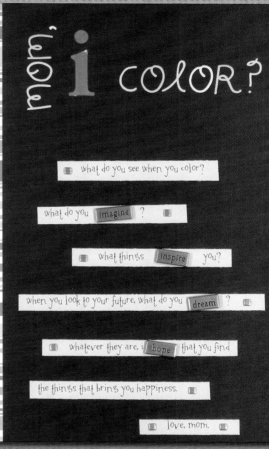

mon, i color?

what do you see when you color?

what do you imagine ?

what things inspire you?

when you look to your future, what do you dream ?

whatever they are, i hope that you find

the things that bring you happiness.

love, mom.

FAVORITE

Gretchen McElveen
of Helena, Alabama

Cardstock: **Bazzill Basics** Paper: **Junkitz** Staples: **Office supply** Ribbon: **Michaels** Tickets: **Party supply** Photo corner and quotation die cuts: **QuicKutz** Letter stickers, pen: **American Crafts**

Add a little metal to a masculine page without adding a lot of bulk – staple in groups of two or three to keep your elements in place. Gretchen added dimension to the white letter stickers by drawing straight lines down some of their edges.

THANKS
Alisha Gordon

Card is 6 x 4 1/2"
Cardstock: **Die Cuts with a View** Paper: **American Crafts** Metal charm, ribbon,
flower: **Making Memories** Ink: **Stampin' Up!**

Set a metal charm in the center of a paper flower, then crumple the petals to
add dimension.

NAP
Brandy Brandon of Layton, Utah

Cardstock, paper, stickers: American Crafts
Brads: **American Crafts, Making Memories**
Bookplate: **Making Memories** Font: **LB Ali-Oops, by Creating Keepsakes**

To create this unique design, adhere patterned paper, a printed quote and two photos on a sheet of cardstock or paper. Trace a circle over the top of them (a large bowl would work well), then cut it out and adhere the piece to the middle of your page. Add large white letter stickers for the title and hold a smaller printed word in place inside a bookplate. Finish by accenting with colored brads.

No day is so bad it can't be fixed by a nap

surrender

NAP

H20 FUN
Tina Gonzales

Paper, stickers: **Creative Imaginations** Metal embellishments: **Making Memories** Die cuts: **Cricut**

Place bright colored metal tokens from Making Memories around your layout for a bit of subtle dimension.

splash   soak up the sun!   lazy days

cooling off

H20 FUN

trip   hot   happy   sun   pool   care free

STITCHED FLORAL

JoAnne Bacon of Alpharetta, Georgia

Cardstock: **Unknown** Paper: **Chatterbox** Decorative brad, ribbon, flowers: **Making Memories** Paint: **Delta**

Dry brush pink acrylic paint over a striped metal frame from Making Memories. Wipe off the excess, leaving paint just in the depressions. Adhere frame to stitched strips of paper on the card front; cut out the middle. Set a decorative metal brad in a pink flower and place inside the card.

COWBOY GIRL
Brandi Barnes of Kelso, Tennessee

Cardstock: **Bazzill Basics** Paper: **Flair Designs, K & Company** Eyelets: **Making Memories** Beads: **The Beadery** Metal photo corners: **K & Company** Flower iron-on appliqués: **Hirschberg Schultz & Co.** Fonts: **Jessie James by Chatterbox, Bickley Script, from fonts.com, Little Trouble Girl, from bvfonts.com**

For a fun western accent, thread beads on leather, knot the ends to keep them in place and hang the piece over a square brad. Brandi journals about sewing her daughters' Halloween costumes each year, so the stitching on this page is especially meaningful.

I am certainly no expert seamstress, but it seems that it has become a tradition for me to make your Halloween costume each year. This year you were a cowgirl (or according to you a "cowboy girl"). Little sister was an Indian and was the perfect sidekick. I joke each year and say that it would be less expensive to buy you a costume by the time I buy the pattern and material, but that just wouldn't be the same now would it? I may not be an expert seamstress, but I could never buy you a costume sewn with more love.

Jewels

jew·el
(jōō'əl) *n.*

1. *the power or quality of pleasing or delighting; a delightful characteristic; a little ornament.*
2. *a small shiny item added to a scrapbook page to increase its attractiveness.*

SIMPLY IRRESISTIBLE

Mary Jo Johnston of West Lafayette, Indiana

Cardstock: **Bazzill Basics** Paper, rhinestone brads, ribbon, stickers, flowers: **Making Memories**
Photo turn: **Creative Impressions** Bottle cap: **Li'l Davis Designs** Rub ons: **Wordsworth**
Photography: **April Kennedy**

Scatter a few flowers around your page and fasten them in place with rhinestone brads.
Create a background for your central photo by mixing ribbon and strips of patterned paper.

PRECIOUS JEWEL
Jeri Hoag of Goshen, Indiana

Cardstock: **Bazzill Basics** Paper: **Chatterbox**
Flowers: **Heidi Swapp** Jewels: **Westrim
Crafts** Stickers: **American Crafts** Circle
template: **Coluzzle** Font: **2Peas Blissful, from**
twopeasinabucket.com

Adhere jewels in a curvy
swirl, starting at the top
of a letter "j" sticker and
finishing just below a
large silk flower. Let the
jewels decrease in size as
you go; create a photo
corner from the leftovers.

Precious **jewel,**
you glow.
you shine.
reflecting all the good things
in this world.
—Maya Angelou

Two hearts...
that belong together.

{a♥k}

TWO HEARTS
Susan Weinroth of Centerville, Minnesota

Cardstock: **Bazzill Basics** Paper: **Fibermark,**
MOD White brad, stickers: **American Crafts**
Rhinestone brads: **SEI** Jewel brads: **SEI** Photo
turns: **7 Gypsies** Font: **2Peas Stop Sign, from**
twopeasinabucket.com

Use rhinestone brads from
SEI as bullets for your printed
sentiment, incorporating them
into a row of brads that goes
down the length of your page.

PRICELESS

Yolanda Williams of Charlotte, North Carolina

Cardstock: **Bazzill Basics** Paper: **Sandylion** Flower transparency: **KI Memories** Metal heart, jewel: **Making Memories** Letter stickers: **My Sticker Studio** Font: **SA Inkspot, from dafont.com**

A single jewel may be all the accent your page needs to make a big statement. Set it on the swirl of a silver heart and adhere the piece to the corner of a matted photo.

BLISS
Cindy Bentley of Allen, Texas

Cardstock, chipboard circle: **Bazzill Basics**
Paper: **MOD** Tags: **Making Memories** Jewels:
Westrim Crafts Lace: **Unknown** Flower, tab:
Heidi Swapp Cardstock stickers: **Sweetwater**
Font: **Uncle Charles by Autumn Leaves**

Adhere jewels in groups of three, setting some over sweet mini tags from Making Memories. The patterned paper from MOD comes with the edges already scalloped; Cindy cut the middle section out and stitched pink cardstock in its place. She also added a Karen Russell border to her photo and had it developed at scrapbookpictures.com.

C & A
Alisha Gordon

Paper: **Making Memories** Metal letters, rub on: **American Crafts** Jewels: **Heidi Swapp** Ribbon: **Lasting Impressions** Ink: **Stampin' Up!**

Stitch a half-circle of patterned paper to the left side of your photo and adhere cut out paisleys to the top and bottom corners on the right side. Visually connect the paisleys with a row of jewels, then knot ribbon around metal monograms for your title.

FRIENDS

Yolanda Williams of Charlotte, North Carolina

Cardstock: **Bazzill Basics** Paper: **Wild Asparagus** Flower brad: **Making Memories** Acrylic flower: **Heidi Swapp** Diamond stickers: **Stampendous** Pen: **Zig** Lettering template: **Scrap Pagerz** Font: **SA Inkspot, from dafont.com**

Scatter jewels on letters and around flower petals to add a touch of glamour to your page. To create her title, Yolanda placed the lettering template over both her torn patterned paper and the cardstock base, traced the letters and colored them in with a colored pencil.

SCIENCE LESSON

Tarri Botwinski
of Grand Rapids, Michigan

Cardstock: **Bazzill Basics** Paper:
Scenic Route Paper Co. Rhinestones:
Craft supply Epoxy stickers: **Creative
Imaginations** Pen: **Marvy Uchida**
Colored pencils: **EK Success** Font: **My
Type of Font**

Cut flowers from patterned
paper — if you don't want to draw
them yourself, trace chipboard
flowers or stickers, or use a die
cut machine. Arrange a group of
five in a corner of your page and
doodle around the edges with a
black pen. Adhere pink and blue
jewels from a craft supply store in
the flower centers and at the ends
of your hand drawn swirls.

I LOVE THIS GIRL

Monica Skeels of Plainfield, Illinois

Cardstock: **Bazzill Basics** Paper: **SEI**
Ribbon slide: **Maya Road** Staples: **Making
Memories** Binder clip: **Li'l Davis Designs**
Rhinestones: **Craft supply** Pen: **Sharpie**

Hearts are the name of the game
in this sweet layout by Monica
Skeels. (Notice how there are even
hearts on the girl's t-shirt in the
photo!) Fill a stitched heart with
pink, red and clear rhinestones
for a dazzling accent; keep them
in place with glue dots or another
strong adhesive. Arrange a circle
of heart patterned paper, the
rhinestone-studded heart and a
photo on black cardstock, then
add a clip and heart ribbon slide
before journaling around the edges
with a white marker.

"S"

Stefanie Hamilton of Lincoln, Nebraska

Paper: **Paper Studio** Rhinestone brads: **Making Memories** Ribbon: **May Arts, Maya Road**
Flowers: **Prima** Acrylic monogram: **Go West Studios** Fabric tape: **7 Gypsies**

Stefanie painted the back of an acrylic monogram pink, then fastened ribbon and a flower at the top. Rhinestone brads hold the ribbon ends in place and add a touch of glamour to this journal cover.

GORGEOUS

Summer Ford
of Bulverde, Texas

Cardstock: **Prism** Paper:
My Mind's Eye Chipboard
flowers: **Everlasting
Keepsakes** Ribbon: **Offray**
Jewels: **Jo-Ann Scrap
Essentials** Rub ons: **Heidi
Grace** Ink: **Stampin'
Up!** Paint: **Plaid** Font:
2Peas Fiori, from
twopeasinabucket.com
Other: **Sand paper, silk leaf**

gorgeous

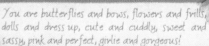

You are butterflies and bows, flowers and frills, dolls and dress up, cute and cuddly, sweet and sassy, pink and perfect, girlie and gorgeous!

Go bold – use a cup or small bowl as a guide for rounding your corners. Summer also cut wavy lines in coordinating paper, layered them across her page and stitched along their curves, bending up the borders for texture.

EVERYDAY JEWELRY

Andie Smith of Deerfield Beach, Florida

Cardstock: **Bazzill Basics** Jewel buckle: **Li'l Davis
Designs** Ribbon: **Unknown** Photo corners:
Close To My Heart Font: **Susie's Hand,** from
momscorner4kids.com

Everyday Jewelry

I love my wedding and engagement ring! After three and half years of marriage I feel naked if I am not wearing it! I wear it everyday. Come to think of it, it is the only jewelry I wear everyday. A lot of the time I forget to put on earrings and a neck lace, or a even a bracelet, but I can't go without my ring. It just seems funny because right after Jason "popped the question" the ring felt funny on my hand. now it's part of me and who I am.

Slide a Li'l Davis jewel buckle over wide pink dotted ribbon to create an accent that's both sweet and elegant.

Organizing!
by Jeri Huish

The world of scrapbooking embellishments is forever changing and expanding. There are always fun new products available that have been designed to add style to our projects. If you're like me, you've happily spent years collecting an enormous hoard of brads, charms, ribbon and trinkets. And before you know it, that collection of brads, charms, ribbon and trinkets is cluttering up rooms of your house. As your collection grows, it becomes more and more important to keep those items easily accessible so they don't become lost, damaged, or forgotten.

So how do you keep this ever-growing, ever-changing collection of small items organized and sorted? Is it possible to accomplish this without spending a small fortune on specialty organizers? Here are a few simple, cost-effective ideas to help arrange and manage your scrapbooking embellishments.

MEDIUM TO SMALL EMBELLISHMENTS

Fishing tackle boxes are the perfect small-embellishment containers. You can purchase these low-cost boxes in the sporting goods section of any large department store. Most are customizable and you can move and arrange dividers and drawers to make large or small compartments, depending on what you're storing inside of them. Use larger drawers for delicate items that need to be flat or protected; such as rub ons, chipboard monograms, tags or blossoms. Save the smaller compartments for charms, letters, acrylic accents, or clips. For tiny items like brads and eyelets, purchase mini-ziplock bags (available at craft stores) and use them to sort your eyelets before stowing them in their own compartment. This will help them stay put if the box is shaken or turned upside down.

FAST TIP: Keep a bottle of adhesive or roll of glue dots in each toolbox so you don't go searching for them each time you get out a box of supplies.

BIG EMBELLISHMENTS

Every husband has an empty tool box stashed somewhere, either a gift, one he's grown out of, or a "spare." Toolboxes are perfect for embellishment storage; they are also inexpensive, convenient to carry and easy to stack and store in a closet or under a table. Snag one of his extras or buy your own and use it for your larger tools and embellishments; staplers, big stamps, ink pads, scissors. Some toolboxes will have a single large compartment; others have smaller, stackable trays. If your collection is really big, consider designating a few toolboxes for different kinds of embellishments; one for stamps, paints and ink, one for pens and adhesives, etc.

FAST TIP: Store your stamp-cleaning supplies along with your stamps to make clean-up easy. If anything is wet or could potentially leak, place it in a ziplock bag just in case.

RIBBON

Coming in a variety of lengths, widths, styles and packaging, ribbon can quickly get out of control. Since it can easily get tangled, dirty or lost just floating around in a drawer somewhere, it is especially important to keep your ribbon organized. An easy way to sort and protect ribbon is to wrap it around an old wrapping paper tube (cut it in half if the whole roll is too bulky). Use a small piece of tape to secure the end, wrap it smoothly around the roll and secure the other end with another piece of tape. I like to write the name and manufacturer of the ribbon right on the cardboard roll for future reference. An added bonus to wrapping your ribbon around something round, rather than a flat, stiff card, is that your ribbon won't come out bent or kinked.

FAST TIP: If your ribbon is wrinkled, run it quickly through a hot curling iron to smooth it out.

PAPER

It's easier to make sense of your paper collection if it's sorted into smaller sections, rather than a giant stack of mismatched sheets. Make sure to organize your paper in a way that makes sense to you. Whether you like it sorted by color, manufacturer or theme, make sure when you buy new paper that you keep your system going and put it away in the right spot.

For 8 1/2 x 11 paper, get a filing box with hanging organizers and sort your paper into the file folders. For the 12 x 12 size, you can invest in a large paper tote, or store paper in the boxes that page protectors come in. Slim and tightly-closing, these will keep your paper organized and clean (although sorting through the stack won't be as convenient as an upright paper tote). You can also store small stacks of paper right in the page protectors themselves; this will keep them flat and clean. There are several paper organizing systems now available, so visit your favorite scrapbook store and see which one would work best for you. I don't think there is anything that will help you more than keeping your scrapbooking paper neatly organized.

FAST TIP: Sort your scraps the same way you sort whole sheets of paper so you'll easily find them later for cards or other projects.

BOOKS

Here is my weakness! Stacks of idea books and magazines teeter on the edges of tables, hide under desks and are tucked away in closets. You can choose to consolidate your collection by tearing out pages with your favorite ideas and arranging them in a 3-ring binder. Or mark your books so finding an idea will be quick and easy. Get several colors of sticky notes and color code them, green for baby ideas, blue for family, red for cool techniques, etc. Attach the sticky note to the page so a tab sticks out and write a quick note to yourself about the idea you liked. The next time you're looking for an idea you can quickly flip through the right tabs, instead of every page. Consider getting some inexpensive plastic magazine holders, or dedicating a shelf of a bookcase to house your collection.

FAST TIP: Occasionally go through your older books. If you flip through an entire book and don't see a single idea that inspires you, give the book away. Don't hold onto things that don't spark your creative energy; the extra bulk will only overwhelm your energy and your storage space.

Most importantly, however you decide to sort and store your supplies, choose a system that works well for you and stick with it. With a little time and effort you can organize your overflowing stockpile of embellishments into a neat and tidy supply. The small monetary investment you might make will actually save you money when you don't lose or ruin items you already have. And the time you spend scrapbooking will be much more fun when you can easily find what you're looking for!

Ruf Ons

Rub on

(rŭb ôn) *n.*

1. to apply pressure; to apply to a surface firmly and with friction.

2. a wide assortment of titles, quotes, alphabets and sayings that can be easily applied to any paper craft; a quick and easy way to make a big statement on your next layout!

Girls CLUB

audrey, this is what you look like when you are mad.

HELP WANTED
ENTER AT YOUR OWN RISK
HANDLE WITH CARE

angry!

MAR 19 2006

ANGRY!

Marci Lambert of Memphis, Tennessee

Cardstock, ink: **Bazzill Basics** Paper: **Design Originals, My Mind's Eye** Transparency: **Daisy D's** Ribbon: **Michaels** Rub ons: **7 Gypsies, Basic Grey, Making Memories** Letter stickers: **American Crafts, Doodlebug Design** Stamp sticker: **Rebecca Sower** Corner rounder: **EK Success** Date stamp: **Memories in the Making** Pen: **Zig** Other: **Vintage ledger paper, netting, staples**

Use a large transparency monogram, such as this one from Daisy D's, to form part of your title. Let a flower rub on peek out from behind your patterned paper photo mat and back a strip of star paper with green netting.

SHE
Heather Thompson of Brentwood, California

Cardstock: **Bazzill Basics** Paper: **Melissa Frances**
Chipboard heart, plastic tag, stickers: **Heidi Swapp**
Rub ons: **Basic Grey** Pen: **Sharpie**

Be dramatic! Apply white floral rub ons from Basic Grey over the entire bottom half of your page to create a beautiful design perfectly in keeping with a girly layout. Heather modified the "she" tag from Heidi Swapp by writing "is" underneath in black pen, then applied another rub on with words that describe her daughter.

MY MCDREAMY
Lizzy Mayorga of Seattle, Washington

Cardstock: **Bazzill Basics** Paper: **Scenic Route Paper Co.** Journaling tag: **7 Gypsies** Jewels: **Hero Arts** Photo corners: **Heidi Swapp** Rub on shapes: **Basic Grey** Rub on letters: **Making Memories** Ink: **Clearsnap** Pen: **Uniball**

Notice how careful placement of the "Love" rub on allows the red patterned paper to show through.

GIRLS JUST WANT TO HAVE FUN

Sybille Moen of Tarzana, California

Cardstock: **Bazzill Basics** Paper, ribbon: **KI Memories** Chipboard monogram: **Basic Grey** Rub ons: **Heidi Swapp, KI Memories**

Apply rub ons directly to your photo to identify the people in it. Apply more rub ons in the shelter of a jumbo chipboard "f" to spell out your title. Sybille covered the Basic Grey monogram in KI Memories patterned paper.

JOURNEY
Kim Hughes of Roy, Utah

Cardstock: **Bazzill Basics** Paper, stickers: **Karen Foster Design** Ribbon: **Unknown** Rub ons: **Royal Brush** Ink: **Stampin' Up!**

Create custom patterned paper by applying various travel-themed rub ons to your background cardstock.

HAPPY SLEEP
Candi Higley of Spanish Fork, Utah

Cardstock: **Provo Craft** Paper: **Scrapworks** Rub ons: **Making Memories** Pen: **Zig**

Use colored rub ons on a black & white photo for a cool effect. Overlap them with smaller, white rub ons to create your title.

COUSINS

Alisha Gordon

Cardstock: **Prism** Paper: **Chatterbox** Rub ons: **American Crafts, Basic Grey** Ribbon: **American Crafts**

Stitch three large blocks of patterned paper to a brown cardstock base. Place your photo in the middle of the page and add jumbo photo corners cut from blue paper. Let two strips of brown ribbon guide your eye to a large rub on title; add rub on flowers as a finishing touch.

CHERISH

Sri Sams of Coral Springs, Florida

Cardstock: **Bazzill Basics** Paper: **A2Z Essentials** Silhouette word: **Heidi Swapp**
Rub ons: **KI Memories** Ink: **Stamp Craft**
Label maker: **Dymo**

Create your caption with a label maker. Print out the words, then cut each one out and stack them to the left of your photo. Apply a grouping of rub on flowers to the top right corner for a pretty accent that also serves to balance your page.

GIRLY

Tina Gonzales

Cardstock, chipboard: **Bazzill Basics**
Paper: **MOD** Ribbon: **May Arts** Rub ons: **KI Memories** Die cuts: **Cricut**

Customize Bazzill Basics chipboard circles by covering them with green paper and applying a pink flower rub on to each one. Line them up across the bottom of your page for a fun, girly accent.

GIRLFRIEND, YOU'RE THE BEST

Liana Suwandi of Wylie, Texas

Card is 4 x 5 1/4"
Pre-made card: **Target** Cardstock: **Bazzill Basics** Paper, rubber frame: **Rob and Bob Studio** Brad: **Chatterbox** Chipboard flower: **Heidi Swapp** Ribbon, sticker: **Making Memories** Rub ons: **Art Warehouse, Doodlebug Design, Karen Foster Design** Circle die cut: **Sizzix** Ink: **Ranger**

Die cut two circles from Rob and Bob Studio patterned paper. Cut about one third from the side of the dotted circle, layer it on the striped circle and stitch them together. Add a large "girlfriend" Art Warehouse rub on, a Heidi Swapp chipboard flower and stitching rub ons from Doodlebug Design.

2ND COUSINS

Clair Moreadith of Ahoskie, North Carolina

Cardstock, paper: **Wild Asparagus** Brads: **Office supply** Chipboard, rub on letters: **Heidi Swapp** Letter stickers: **Bo-Bunny Press, Chatterbox** Die cut photo corners: **QuicKutz** Pens: **LePlume, Zig**

Clair began by drawing the flourish designs by hand on either side of her page, then added a strip of red cardstock and green dotted paper. She journaled next to the photo, then added chipboard letters and an ampersand sticker above the journaling. The title was created with red Bo-Bunny Press letter stickers and black Heidi Swapp rub ons.

HAPPY GIRL

Jamie Cottrell of Sullivan, Missouri

Cardstock, chipboard: **Bazzill Basics** Paper, die cuts, stickers: **MOD** Ric rac: **Doodlebug Design** Rub ons: **Making Memories, MOD** Paint: **Making Memories** Pen: **Pigment Pro**

Jamie used a large pre-cut patterned paper flower from MOD as a creative base for her page. She adhered strips of paper and blue ric rac across the middle, along with an off-set photo, before journaling around the edges of the flower. Large rub on letters from Making Memories make the title, while smaller, colorful rub ons from MOD create interest in the bottom right corner of the photo. Notice how Jamie added small MOD epoxy stickers over the letters in "girl"; she also covered three Bazzill Basics chipboard squares with patterned paper, inked the edges and adhered them below her photo.

Ribbon

rib·bon

(rĭb'ən) *n.*

1. *a narrow strip or band of fine fabric, finished at the edges and used for trimming, tying or finishing.*
2. *one of the hottest embellishments in the world of scrapbooking; a perfect addition to any project.*

A HINT OF HAYDEN

Jamie Cottrell of Sullivan, Missouri

Cardstock: **Bazzill Basics** Rhinestone brads, ribbon, buttons, paint: **Making Memories** Flower: **Heidi Swapp** Chipboard: **Basic Grey** Pen: **Pigment Pro**

Ribbon bullets! These ingenious accents in pink and green add color and pizzazz to a girly layout. Hold the small tabs in place with small rhinestone brads from Making Memories.

TASTE OF SUMMER
Heather Thompson of Brentwood, California

Cardstock: **Bazzill Basics** Paper: **Basic Grey, Making Memories, MOD, Rusty Pickle** Brad: **Chatterbox** Embroidery floss: **DMC** Ribbon: **Michaels** Ric rac: **Unknown** Rub ons: **K & Company** Ink: **Ranger** Fonts: **Migraine Serif, Swish Buttons, both from dafont.com, Secrets, from girlswhowearglasses.com, Decker**

Crisscross two small pieces of ribbon for a unique photo corner; hand stitch it in place. Hand stitch wide yellow ric rac with black embroidery floss for subtle texture. Heather created the tag herself by overlapping text and dingbats and changing the colors.

BACKPACK
Sandi Hicks of San Antonio, Texas

Cardstock: **Bazzill Basics** Paper: **Scenic Route Paper Co.** Ribbon: **American Crafts** Flower: **Imagination Project** Chipboard arrow: **Basic Grey** Chipboard letters: **Heidi Swapp**

Use ribbon to underscore your title; knot the same ribbon around a chipboard arrow that points to a key part of your photo. A small chipboard flower between two of your title letters is a sweet finishing touch.

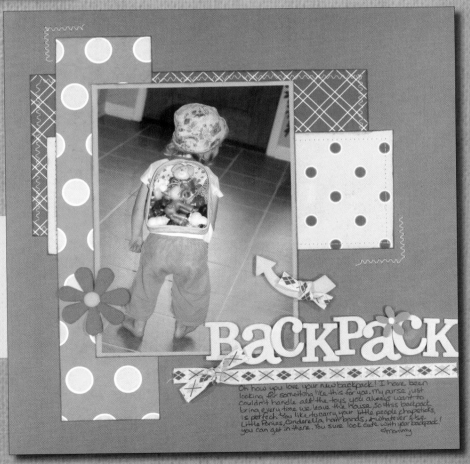

you love to stand at the long antique table and set up your little playmobile people and all your little plastic animals for hours just feeling the sun light fall upon your face, and i sit and listen to your baby chatter trying to make sense of your world as i smile focus and capture you forever

AGE 2

Tara Pakosta of Libertyville, Illinois

Cardstock: **Bazzill Basics** Paper: **Bo-Bunny Press** Stick pin, jewels, ribbon, sweetheart tag: **Making Memories** Flower: **Chatterbox** Chipboard photo corner: **Chatterbox** Rub ons: **Autumn Leaves** Stamps: **Hero Arts** Chalk ink: **ColorBox**

Fasten a tag and flower in place with a stick pin at the intersection of two lengths of ribbon.

SUGAR & SPICE

Summer Fullerton of Tigard, Oregon

Cardstock: **Memories Forever** Paper, ribbon, rub ons, stickers: **Arctic Frog** Stick pin: **Boxer** Stamps: **Provo Craft, Technique Tuesday** Ink: **StazOn**

Arrange seven or eight ribbons of varying widths across the middle of your page. Notch the left ends and use them as a mat for your photo. Finish with stamped brackets from Technique Tuesday and a title made from rub ons and stickers.

SUSAN

Kelly Purkey of Chicago, Illinois

Cardstock: **Bazzill Basics** Brads, ribbon, stickers: **American Crafts** Pen: **Signo Uniball** Photography: **Becky Cantu**

Adhere bits of ribbon in a colorful array around your matted photo; secure some ends with brads and adhere the rest. Color makes a big impact on a black cardstock background – journal with a gel pen around your border for a creative finishing touch.

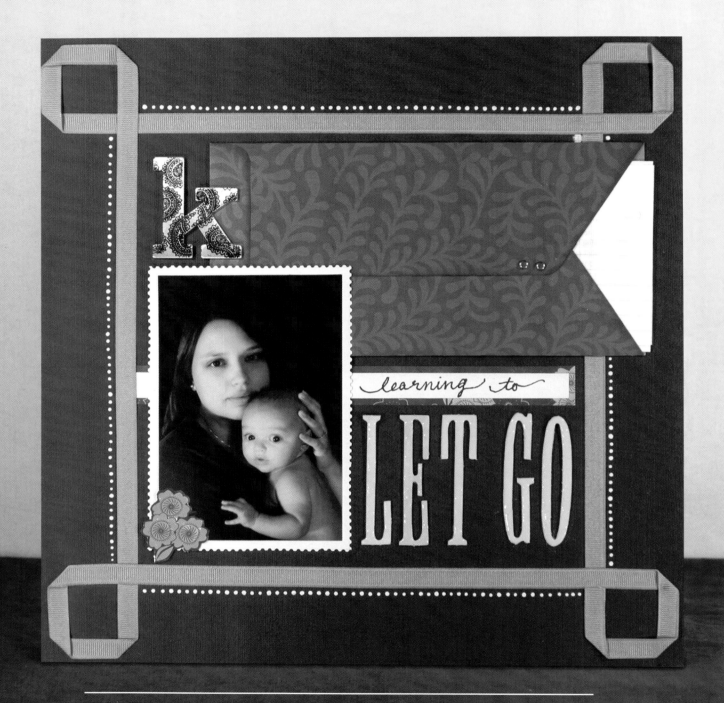

LEARNING TO LET GO

Kara Henry

Cardstock: **Bazzill Basics** Paper: **Die Cuts with a View, Keeping Memories Alive** Metal monogram, brads, chipboard letters: **Making Memories** Ribbon, stamp: **Craft supply** Scissors: **Fiskars** Ink: **Tsukineko** Pen: **American Crafts** Paint: **Delta** Dimensional adhesive: **Diamond Glaze**

Use a long length of ribbon to create this intricate border – use a bit of double-sided tape to hold it in place as you work. Adhere the ribbon ends under your journaling pocket and add a metal monogram covered in paisley paper. The flowers in the corner of the photo are hand cut from a sheet of patterned paper from Keeping Memories Alive.

I LOVE RIBBON

Candi Higley of Spanish Fork, Utah

Cardstock: **Bazzill Basics, Provo Craft**
Ribbon: **American Crafts, Offray, Making
Memories, unknown** Stickers: **American
Crafts** Ink: **Tsukineko**

In an all-about-me album,
make a layout about your
favorite embellishments. Of
course, you'll want to use
them on the page itself!

THIS SWEET FACE

Kim Moreno of Tucson, Arizona

Cardstock: **Bazzill Basics** Paper, ribbon,
stickers: **American Crafts** Brads: **Making
Memories** Photo turns: **7 Gypsies**
Chipboard heart, photo corners: **Heidi
Swapp** Circle punch: **Creative Memories**
Pen: **Sakura** Font: **Micahels Plain, from
searchfreefonts.com**

Tie two photo turns together
with striped ribbon; knot the
same ribbon around the bottom
of your journaling block.

I love your long
beautiful eyelashes and
your big brown eyes.
Your sweet little lips
that pucker up so cute
to give me smooches.
Your cheeks that used
to have some chub to
them now look more
like little boy cheeks
rather than baby
cheeks. You are my
sweet baby boy and I
love your sweet face.

Today the girls went back to school. With Lexi being in school all day now, this means I only have one left at home. Just one. Just one to take care of. Just one to feed lunch. Just one to play with. Just one to talk to. Just one to keep me occupied. Just one to drive me batty. Just one.

At least until the weekend comes.

8.24.05

AND THEN THERE WAS ONE

Barbara Pfeffer of Omaha, Nebraska

Paper, stickers: **Arctic Frog** Brads: **American Crafts** Ribbon: **Bazzill Basics, Li'l Davis Designs, Offray** Circle template: **Coluzzle** Fonts: **Arial, Verdana**

Use a circle template to cut semi-circles to place in the corners of your layout; zigzag stitch them in place. Fold bits of coordinating ribbon in half, trim the ends and secure them to the page with brads. You can prevent the ribbon from pulling by piercing a hole in the ribbon with a needle before you push the brad through.

UNCOOPERATIVE

Celeste Smith
of West Hartford, Connecticut

Cardstock: **Bazzill Basics** Paper:
Anna Griffin Brad: **Jo-Ann Essentials**
Ribbon: **Unknown** Mesh: **Magic**
Mesh Letter stickers: **Chatterbox**
Pen: **Sakura**

To create this charming flower
accent (that goes great with the
Anna Griffin patterned paper at
the bottom of the page) begin
with three 6" lengths of ribbon.
Fold the ends of each one under
so they meet in the middle; adhere
the ends in place. Stack the folded
ribbon to create a flower with six
petals; set a large brad through the
center to keep the ribbon together.

Keep your leftover bits of ribbon!
When you have enough pieces, gather
them in colors that match the paper
you're using and stack them down the
left side of your page. Add interest
with pins, staples, ribbon slides,
buttons and by knotting the ribbon.
Amy used an x-acto knife to hand
cut the letters from chipboard, then
covered them with brown paper from
Chatterbox before sanding the edges.

AMY

Amy Williams of Spanish Fork, Utah

Cardstock: **Bazzill Basics** Paper: **Chatterbox**
Safety pins: **Making Memories** Ribbon
charms: **KI Memories** Ribbon: **American**
Crafts, May Arts Other: **Buttons,**
chipboard, staples

Flowers

flow·er

(flou'ᵊr) *n.*

1. *a plant that is cultivated or appreciated for its blossoms; having showy or colorful parts; a blossom.*
2. *a very fun touch for cards and layouts; available in every color and style imaginable.*

SILLY, FUNNY, CRAZY CUTE
SILLY, FUNNY, CRAZY CUTE

SILLY, FUNNY, CRAZY CUTE
Monica Schoenemann of Flower Mound, Texas

Cardstock: **Bazzill Basics, Die Cuts with a View** Paper: **American Crafts** Buttons: **Foof-a-La, Lasting Impressions, Making Memories** Chipboard heart, letter stickers: **Making Memories** Flowers: **Doodlebug Design, Prima** Pens: **Signo, Zig** Font: **Tahoma**

Cut flowers from patterned paper and arrange them in a wide curve across the bottom of your page. Add paper flowers from Doodlebug Design and tiny buttons along the edges. Monica doodled underneath the flowers with black pen to create a cool retro look.

A NEW ME
Becky Novacek of Fremont, Nebraska

Paper: **Anna Griffin, Basic Grey, Chatterbox, Foof-a-La, Melissa Frances, MOD** Index tab: **7 Gypsies** Flowers: **Prima** Rub ons: **Making Memories** Bracket stamps: **Green Grass Stamps** Ink: **ColorBox** Pen: **American Crafts** Other: **Jewels, thread**

Choose patterned papers with floral designs, cut them into blocks and stack them up the left side of your page. Stamp your title in one of the blocks and break up the middle line with a photo. Stitch around the edge.

LOVE AND JOY
Courtney Kelly of Colorado Springs, Colorado

Cardstock: **Bazzill Basics** Paper: **Scenic Route Paper Co.** Brads, ribbon: **American Crafts** Flower, photo corners: **Heidi Swapp** Wood tag: **Basic Grey** Font: **Tin Birdhouse,** from dafont.com

Let a wooden tag be the center of your flower, then place various sized brads coming away from the flower around the photo. Stagger your journaling strips to break up the lines of the photo mat.

You bring a new special love to my life and to our family. You have such a gift of making people smile. I love you and I hope we can give you the same love that you bring to us. Love, Daddy.

YOU

Courtney Kelly of Colorado Springs, Colorado

Cardstock: **Bazzill Basics** Paper, brad: **American Crafts** Fabric flower, chipboard flower: **Heidi Swapp**
Paper flower: **Making Memories** Fabric tab: **Scrapworks** Font: **Century Gothic**

Layer a light pink paper flower from Making Memories over a darker pink Heidi Swapp chipboard flower, then fasten them together with a brad. Place the piece over the bottom right corner of your photo; position a larger silk flower part way behind the photo's left side to create balance.

NOTHING ELSE MATTERS

Monica Schoenemann
of Flower Mound, Texas

Cardstock, die cut flowers: **KI Memories**
Paper: **Provo Craft** Fibers: **Making
Memories** Buttons: **Foof-a-La** Pen:
Signo Fonts: Playground and Gift, both
from twopeasinabucket.com

Set buttons in the center of
die cut flowers after hand
stitching stems in green. Let
the flowers span an entire side
of your page for a big impact.

You two are my life.

You are my forever loves.

You make me laugh to no end

You are happy, and you make me happy

You are healthy as healthy can be

You are my hopes for the future.

You are my dreams for life ever after

You are my everything

nothing else matters!

WHISPER

Tina Albertson of Harlan, Indiana

Cardstock: **Bazzill Basics** Decorative tape,
chipboard letters, photo corners, jewels, acrylic
flowers, fabric flowers, puffy stickers: **Heidi
Swapp** Pen: **Zig**

Layer acrylic flowers,
fabric flowers and puffy
green stickers to create
a pretty floral trio along
the top of your layout.
Sand the edges of green
chipboard letters and
add an ellipsis with
jewel stickers.

BLOOM AND GROW
Pam Callaghan of Bowling Green, Ohio

Cardstock: **Bazzill Basics** Paper, die cuts, letters: **3 Bugs in a Rug** Brads: **Making Memories** Decorative metal charm: **Karen Foster Design** Ribbon: **American Crafts, Doodlebug Design, May Arts, SEI** Paper flowers: **Prima** Buttons: **Unknown** Rub ons: **Gin-X**
Ink: **Ranger** Pen: **Zig**

Arrange curvy strips of green paper on the right side of your page to create the stems for this bouquet of paper flowers. Tie ribbon around the middle before stitching them in place. Cut out flowers from paper and adhere to the top; add buttons and brads to their centers. Rub ons applied to light green paper make the leaves.

SWEET THING

Doris Sander of Hermitage, Tennessee

Cardstock: **Bazzill Basics** Paper: **American Crafts, Scenic Route Paper Co.** Silk flowers, chipboard heart, photo corner: **Heidi Swapp** Ribbon: **Heidi Swapp, Making Memories** Pens: **Sharpie, Zig** Other: **Rhinestones**

Adhere strips of patterned paper at angles down the left side of your page and align your journaling with the slant. Use rhinestones to embellish the centers of both silk flowers and the flowers on the patterned paper. Add a trio of rhinestones next to a Heidi Swapp chipboard heart.

YOU ROCK

Katrina Simeck
of Colchester, Vermont

Cardstock: **Bazzill Basics** Paper: **Urban Lily** Brads: **Jo-Ann Essentials** Bookplate: **Making Memories** Flowers: **Prima** Letter stickers: **American Crafts** Font: **Minya Nouvelle, from 1001fonts.com**

Cut a large curve from a sheet of flowery Urban Lily patterned paper and adhere it to your base piece of tan cardstock. Set pink paper flowers along the seam with brads; add another flower next to your title.

BEAUTY

Jeri Huish

Paper: **Scenic Route Paper Co. (green dots & brown floral)**, **Wild Asparagus (cream & red floral)**, **Chatterbox (solid green)** Brads: **Bazzill Basics** Flowers: **Bazzill Basics and Forever Flowers** Ribbon: **SEI and May Arts** Stickers: **Wild Asparagus** Font: **MA Simple Pleasures, from dafont.com** Pen: **Zig** Ink: **Ranger** Photography: **Amanda Fillerup**

Layer paper flowers over silk flowers; fasten them together with a brad and scatter them around your page for a soft, feminine feel. Jeri outlined the die cut letters with a brown pen to help them stand out against the patterned paper.

XO
Ali McLaughlin of Bristow, Virginia

Cardstock: **Bazzill Basics** Paper, stickers: **Christina Cole** Chipboard flowers: **Gin-X** Chipboard letters: **We R Memory Keepers** Font: **SP Miss Purkey, from scrapsupply.com**

Set Christina Cole epoxy stickers in the center of Gin-X chipboard flowers for colorful accents that look great scattered across the bottom of your page. Use them to hold small printed journaling blocks in place.

these days we seem to butt heads...

But I still Love ya Attitude And all...

XO

my favorite thing about you...

your sweetness

there is no sweeter girl as far as I know you bring your smile where-ever you go you pick me flowers, you dance, you sing you really are the sweetest thing

SWEETNESS
Heather Thompson of Brentwood, Califonia

Cardstock: **Bazzill Basics** Paper, rub ons: **Melissa Frances** Buttons: **Bluementhal Lansing Co.** Jewels: **Westrim Craft** Flower: **Craft Supply** Marker: **Sharpie**

Stitch stems in curvy lines up one side of your page and place silk flowers at the top of the stems. Glue buttons, jewels or even pearls in the flower centers.

Brads

---

brad

(brăd) *n.*

1. a thin wire nail with a small head.
2. a fun embellishment used to mount titles, tags, journaling and more; brads can be petite or bold, unobtrusive or used to add a big splash of color and style.

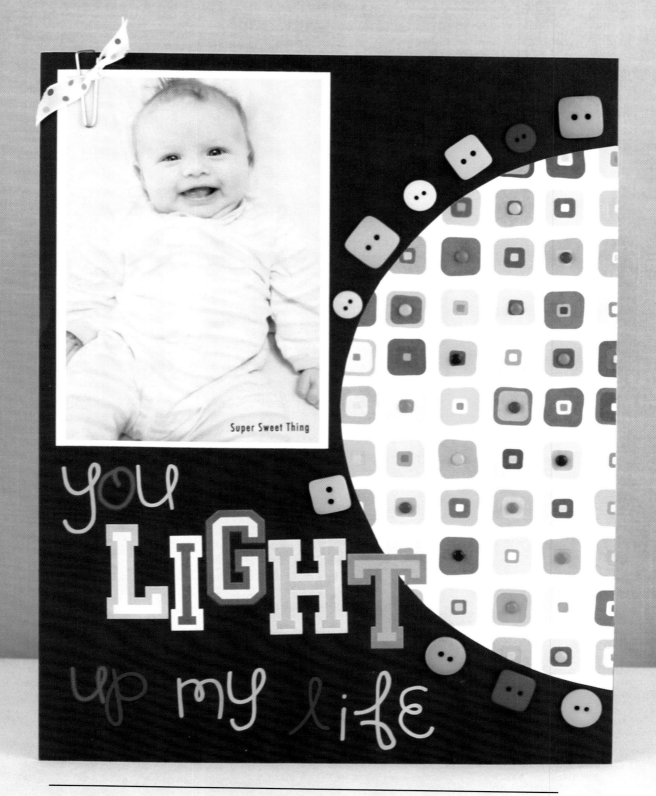

Super Sweet Thing

you LIGHT up my life

YOU LIGHT UP MY LIFE
Kristina Proffitt of Huntsville, Alabama

Cardstock: **Bazzill Basics** Paper: **KI Memories** Brads: **Making Memories** Ribbon: **Fibers By the Yard** Buttons: **American Crafts, unknown** Rub ons: **Basic Grey** Stickers: **American Crafts, KI Memories** Other: **Paperclip**

Set circle brads in the center of squares on your patterned paper. Continue the circle/square theme by cutting the paper into a semi-circle and accenting your page with circle and square buttons and polka dot ribbon.

10 THINGS I LOVE ABOUT YOU
Cheryl Manz of Paulding, Ohio

Paper: **American Crafts, KI Memories** Brads, letter stickers: **American Crafts** Acrylic hearts and letters: **Heidi Swapp** Flower stamp: **Hero Arts** Ink: **StazOn**

Print things you love about a friend on patterned paper, cut into strips, then arrange them in an hourglass pattern on your page. Use colored brads as bullets for each item. Stamp a flower several times in the bottom corner of your photo, stamping off the edge for an artistic look.

GIRL FRIENDS
Alisha Gordon

Cardstock, paper, tags, ribbon: **SEI** Brads: **SEI, Lasting Impressions** Flowers: **Queen & Co.** Chipboard letters: **Heidi Swapp** Pen: **Zig** Ink: **Stampin' Up!**

Set large brads through acrylic flowers; group three of them next to your title. Use smaller brads to set tags in place, creating a mat for your photo.

FLOWERS
Kelly Purkey of Chicago, Illinois

Card is 5 1/2 x 4"
Cardstock: **Bazzill Basics** Paper, brads: **American Crafts** Stamps: **Fontwerks** Ink: **StazOn**

Glue a piece of dotted paper across the bottom of a dark blue card base; stamp flowers on colored paper and cut out. Choose brads in an assortment of colors that match your paper, then use them to fasten the stamped flowers across the seam.

KJ
Julie Laakso of Howell, Michigan

Cardstock: **Bazzill Basics** Paper: **Scenic Route Paper Co.** Brads: **American Crafts** Ribbon: **Craft supply** Chipboard letters: **Li'l Davis Designs** Rub ons: **Doodlebug Design** Ink: **Marvy Uchida** Fonts: **Script by Creating Keepsakes, Times New Roman**

Create a photo corner from seven evenly spaced black brads, like these from American Crafts. Julie cut wavy lines from her patterned paper, then matted the paper on black cardstock. She also added a floral border to the pink paper with rub on flowers from Doodlebug Design.

Ah, baby girl... you've only been with us for three and a half weeks and I already wonder what it was like without you.

LEARN
Heather Thompson of Brentwood, California

Cardstock: **Bazzill Basics** Paper, letterbrads, file folder: **Rusty Pickle** White brad, paint: **Making Memories** Chipboard photo turn: **Basic Grey** Stickers: **American Crafts** Pens: **American Crafts, Sharpie** Glaze: **Judikins** Other: **Notebook paper**

Heather colored the alphabet brads from Rusty Pickle with paint pens, then coated them with Diamond Glaze – a great way to match your embellishments to your paper. She used blue acrylic paint on the chipboard photo turn and paint pens to create the border on the file folder and the dotted borders.

grace - age 4½

She can write all her letters & she's starting to ask how to spell things. her favorite thing to write is her name!

HOWDY
Tina Gonzales

Card is 4 x 6"
Cardstock: **Bazzill Basics** Brads: **Eyelet Warehouse** Ribbon: **May Arts** Die cuts: **Cricut** Stamps, ink: **Close To My Heart**

Stamp a pocket on white cardstock, cut out. Set brads in the corners for an authentic looking accent.

QUESTION MARK
Sarah Klemish of Midland, Michigan

Cardstock: **Bazzill Basics** Paper, brads:
American Crafts Chipboard question mark:
Heidi Swapp Font: **Bell Gothic**

Use large brads, such as
these yellow ones from
American Crafts, to
accent circles on a strip
of patterned paper that
spans your page.

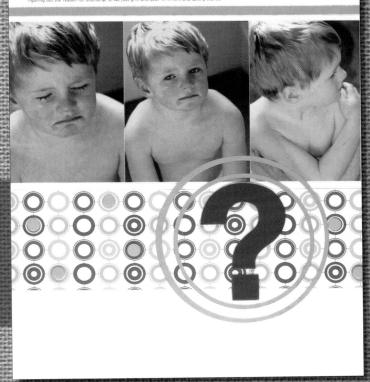

Minute by minute, hour by hour, day to day......we never know when the ''H Bomb'' is going to hit. Most of the time we have a hard time figuring out the reason for discharge so we just grin and bear it .....Oh, and take pictures.

DOODLE
Alecia Grimm of Atlanta, Georgia

Cardstock: **Bazzill Basics** Paper, letter
stickers: **Sonburn** Brads: **Making
Memories** Font: **2Peas Happy Go Lucky**,
from twopeasinabucket.com

Juxtapose black and white
patterned paper on your page;
alternate pieces of black and white
paper to create a frame. Notice how
the green title letters add a punch
of color that echoes the green shirt
in the photo. Alecia used gem
brads from Making Memories as
bullets for her journaling.

LOVE YA
Tammy Morrill

Card is 4 1/4 x 5 1/2"
Cardstock: **Provo Craft** Paper: **Making Memories** Rhinestone brad: **SEI** Matte brads, ribbon:
Lasting Impressions "Love ya" stamp: **Green Grass Stamps** Ink: **StazOn**

Stamp a small sentiment on white cardstock, trim to a rectangle and punch a 1/8" hole at
the top. Tie it to velvet ribbon amid a cluster of flowers held in place with colored brads.
When adding velvet to a project, make sure your placement is just right before you adhere
it to the paper. Once it's in place, moving it can tear out the fuzz.

A LITTLE BIT SASSY
Sandi Hicks of San Antonio, Texas

Cardstock, jumbo brads: **Bazzill Basics** Paper: **Basic Grey** Ribbon: **May Arts** Chipboard "s": **We R Memory Keepers** Chipboard heart and letters: **Heidi Swapp** Rub ons: **Imagination Project** Paint: **Making Memories**

Sandi used chipboard letters from two companies, so she painted them all to make them uniform. Notice how she used her photo to inspire her color and paper choices – the aqua of her daughter's shirt can be seen in the painted letters and jumbo brads, while the floral pattern on her daughter's do-rag is reflected in the floral patterned paper.

SHE
Mary MacAskill
of Calgary, Alberta, Canada

Cardstock: **Bazzill Basics** Paper: **Sassafras Lass** Brads: **Making Memories** Flower charms: **Nunn Designs** Buttons: **Foof-a-La** Stickers: **American Crafts** Pen: **Sharpie** Font: **Steelfish**, from dafont.com

Choose phrases that describe a friend and print them, leaving room at the left for a brad. Print the last phrase on colored paper for a dramatic effect. Stagger the strips on the edge of a photo, then add colored letter stickers to the top left corner. Mary cut the "{simply}" from American Crafts Simply Chic letter packaging.

HOT
NEW
embellishments

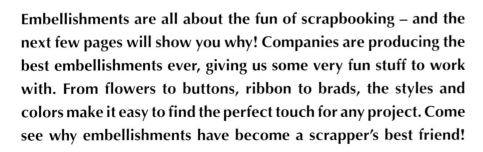

Embellishments are all about the fun of scrapbooking – and the next few pages will show you why! Companies are producing the best embellishments ever, giving us some very fun stuff to work with. From flowers to buttons, ribbon to brads, the styles and colors make it easy to find the perfect touch for any project. Come see why embellishments have become a scrapper's best friend!

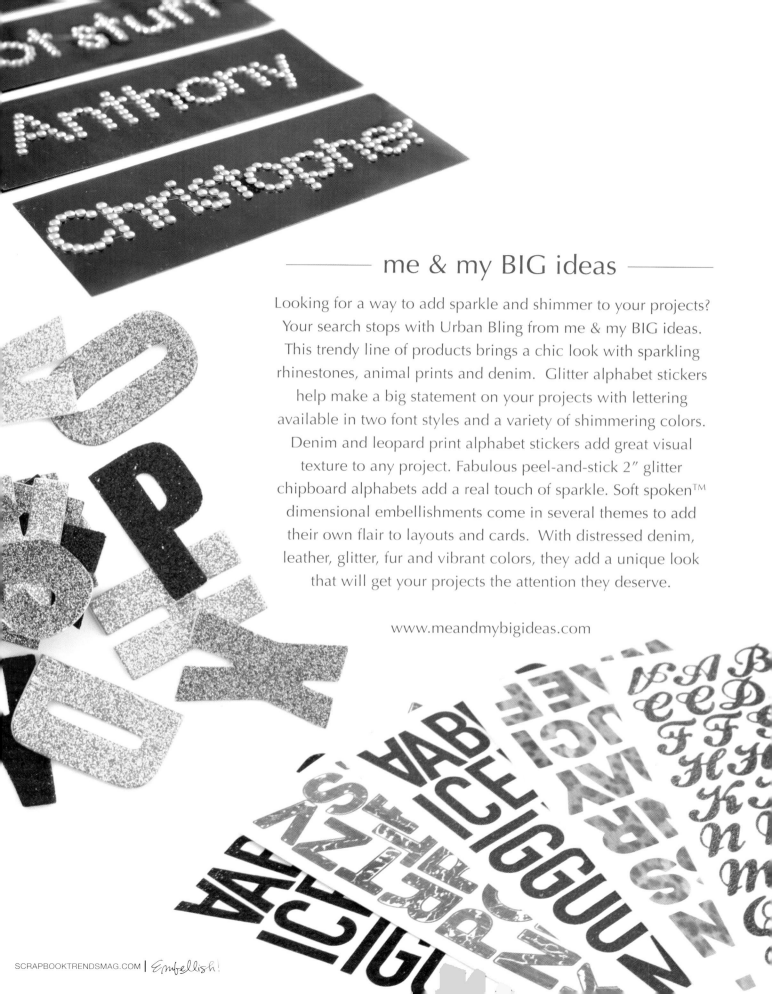

me & my BIG ideas

Looking for a way to add sparkle and shimmer to your projects? Your search stops with Urban Bling from me & my BIG ideas. This trendy line of products brings a chic look with sparkling rhinestones, animal prints and denim. Glitter alphabet stickers help make a big statement on your projects with lettering available in two font styles and a variety of shimmering colors. Denim and leopard print alphabet stickers add great visual texture to any project. Fabulous peel-and-stick 2" glitter chipboard alphabets add a real touch of sparkle. Soft spoken™ dimensional embellishments come in several themes to add their own flair to layouts and cards. With distressed denim, leather, glitter, fur and vibrant colors, they add a unique look that will get your projects the attention they deserve.

www.meandmybigideas.com

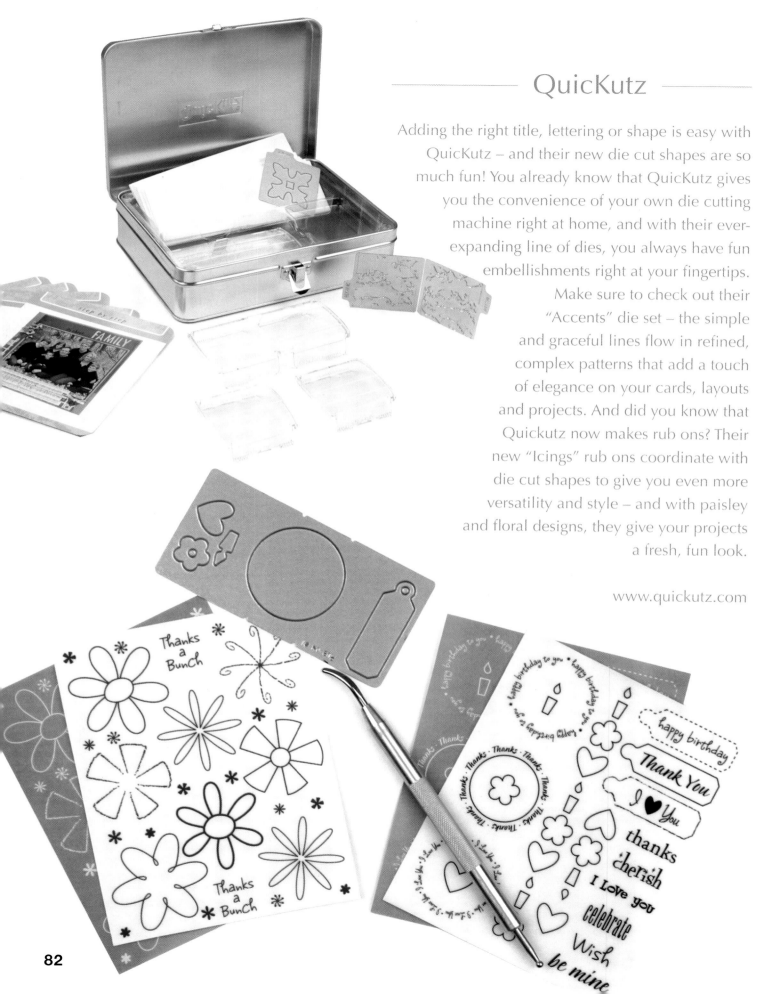

QuicKutz

Adding the right title, lettering or shape is easy with QuicKutz – and their new die cut shapes are so much fun! You already know that QuicKutz gives you the convenience of your own die cutting machine right at home, and with their ever-expanding line of dies, you always have fun embellishments right at your fingertips. Make sure to check out their "Accents" die set – the simple and graceful lines flow in refined, complex patterns that add a touch of elegance on your cards, layouts and projects. And did you know that Quickutz now makes rub ons? Their new "Icings" rub ons coordinate with die cut shapes to give you even more versatility and style – and with paisley and floral designs, they give your projects a fresh, fun look.

www.quickutz.com

Thank heaven for little girls
Alan Jay Lerner

I think that I see something deeper, more infinite, more eternal than the ocean in the expression of the eyes of a little baby.
Vincent Van Gogh

sweetheart

wild·asparagus™

Approx. 36 inches (1 yard) of ribbon

darling bo

baby boy

ALL BO

Look! how he laughs and stretches out his arms, and opens wide his eyes upon thine while his little form flutters as winged with joy.

My Mind's Eye

Between the beautiful, vintage "Wild Asparagus" and the fun, colorful "Kaleidoscope" lines from My Mind's Eye, you're bound to find the perfect combination of products to put together amazing scrapbook pages. Matching frames, borders, tags, terrific alphabet stickers - not to mention coordinating flowers and ribbon - mean you get everything you need for professional looking pages that are a breeze to put together. Gorgeous patterns are printed on heavy, textured cardstock so you can rest easy knowing you're preserving your memories with high quality, as well as stylish, products.

www.mymindseyeinc.com

dad

grat

wish
/wish/ verb

gra

Thankful

ppreciate

reasure

thanksgiving

Doodlebug Design

Looking for some fun new embellishments? We just couldn't wait to get our hands on the new products from Doodlebug Design! These buttons, flowers, ribbons and clips - in all the hottest new colors - are going to add life and excitement to your latest projects. Striped buttons make it easy to stitch cuteness to your cards, tags and layouts, plus they coordinate perfectly with the striped grosgrain ribbon. If you need just the right assortment of buttons, they come in custom colors in packages of 24 and include polka dot, frost and glitter style buttons. And of course, these beautiful silk flowers will have you smiling as they help you add a touch of fun to anything you make. And don't miss out on the "Cute Clips", available in several themes. These great products from Doodlebug Design are the latest and greatest way to add color, dimension and warmth to your paper creations!

www.doodlebug.ws

Making Memories

The hottest home décor and fashion trends join with scrapbooking styles to bring us fun products that are pure pleasure to create with! This has never been more true than with the Boho Chic line of embellishments by Making Memories. This hip style translates into limitless paper creations. "Our Boho Chic programs are all about releasing your inner gypsy," explains Making Memories Product Manager Stacy Boothe. Mini albums and brad accents are just the beginning. Crystal brads are sure to become one of your very favorite new toys. Beautiful metal frames and accessories are also available, with distressed paint and beautifully aged copper finishes. Soft embellishments include ric rac, crocheted lace trims, woven ribbons and more. Other great new embellishments are colorboard stickers, available in 13 popular themes. Constructed from sturdy die-cut chipboard, this fun new collection includes tags, frames, ribbon slides and more.

www.makingmemories.com

Karen Foster Design

We are all in love with jumbo ric rac by Karen Foster Design! This extra-wide ric rac is such a fun addition to your stash of favorite finds. It is a perfect accent piece and comes in a wide array of colors. And when you think of brads, you are sure to think of Karen Foster. Ribbon brads are fun to use with scrapper's floss to loop and lace on your project, and can also be used for hanging charms or other embellishments. And don't miss out on the fun new zig zag brads – perfect for underlining words, framing photos or journaling, decorating corners, and more. Other innovative and fun embellishments are the corner and frame brads, macaroni brads and round and square biggie brads. If you are looking for something to enhance your latest project, Karen Foster has the perfect solution.

www.karenfosterdesign.com

Acrylic

a·cryl·ic
(ə-krĭl'ĭk) *n.*

1. *a glassy thermoplastic; can be cast and molded or used in coatings and adhesives; used especially by artists.*
2. *particularly useful in the art of scrapbooking, acrylic embellishments are a versatile way to add subtle color and texture to a layout or card.*

ME

Alexis Hardy of Franklin Square, New York

Cardstock: **Bazzill Basics** Paper: **Basic Grey, Cherry Arte, Kaleidoscope** Love tag: **Making Memories** Acrylic letters, chipboard heart, decorative tape: **Heidi Swapp** Die cuts: **Kaleidoscope** Rub ons: **Heidi Swapp, Scrapworks, Scenic Route Paper Co.** Stickers: **KI Memories, Making Memories, me & my BIG ideas** Ink: **StazOn** 3-D paint: **Duncan Scribbles** Pens: **Sigma, Zig** Font: **Times New Roman** Other: **Bird cut-out**

Create a layout about yourself using this fresh take on speech balloons. Cut each balloon from patterned paper and rotate them out from the center. Place a photo of yourself in one and words and images that describe you in the rest. (Notice how the bird cut out echoes the design on Alexis' shirt!) Edge Heidi Swapp acrylic "ghost letters" with white paint for your title, then adhere them over a strip of dotted paper – with some careful placement, the dots can be used to disguise dabs of glue. *P.S. Think you can't draw a speech bubble? Start with a rectangle, round the corners, then draw a triangle-ish shape coming from one corner. Easy!*

GONNA GETCHA
Shelby Valadez of Saugus, California

Cardstock: **Pebbles, Inc.** Paper: **Scenic Route Paper Co.** Acrylic letters: **KI Memories** Chipboard letters and heart: **Heidi Swapp** Ink: **Marvy Uchida** Font: **Century Gothic**

Using two patterned papers, cut six rectangles, ink the edges and stack them on the left side of your page. Add strips of black cardstock and a matted photo. Place red acrylic letters vertically over the patterned paper and a chipboard heart at the bottom right of the photo. Place Heidi Swapp chipboard letters face down on patterned paper, trace and cut out. Ink the edges black and adhere them to the chipboard. Print your journaling in red and trim out into small strips.

LIVE 2 LAUGH
Nichole Pereira of Santa Clara, California

Cardstock: **Bazzill Basics** Paper: **My Mind's Eye** Brads: **American Crafts** Acrylic letters: **Heidi Swapp** Tags: **Li'l Davis Designs** Pen: **Staedtler** Font: **Century Gothis**

Stack two photos on the left side of your page; let them extend from the top to the bottom. Mat flowered paper on dotted paper, round the right-hand corners of each piece and place on your page. Print your journaling on a pink tag and stagger two more tags to back your title. "Live" and "laugh" are Heidi Swapp acrylic letters, while the number 2 is an SEI sticker that has been traced on a blue circle. Add a Heidi Swapp "sweetie" tab to the left side of your top photo.

SISTERS
Kay Rogers of Midland, Michigan

Cardstock: **Bazzill Basics** Paper, acrylic embellishments, stickers: **KI Memories** Brads: **Die Cuts with a View** Ribbon: **Making Memories** Rub ons: **Doodlebug Design** Pen: **Zig**

Cut a wavy line from striped paper, then adhere it to the bottom half of your page. Spell out your title with a mix of die cuts, stickers and pink acrylic letters. Put an acrylic frame to good use along a strip of patterned paper; the square acrylic token inside matches up with the pattern. Knot ribbon through an acrylic heart tag and use it to accent the corner of a black & white photo. Apply stitching rub ons from Doodlebug Design in key places on your layout and journal along the top edge of the striped paper.

ORIGINAL
Doris Sander of Hermitage, Tennessee

Cardstock: **Bazzill Basics** Paper: **MOD** Ribbon: **American Crafts, KI Memories, Michaels** Acrylic letters: **KI Memories** Chipboard frame: **Li'l Davis Designs** Pen: **Zig** Quote: **Autumn Leaves Quote book** Photography: **Lisa Truesdell** Other: **Sequins, rhinestones, staples**

Arrange a cheerful mix of acrylic letters in a curvy line to create your title, then incorporate the word into a handwritten quote or journaling. Write a caption for your photo on colored paper and place it behind a chipboard frame.

I LOVE THIS FACE
Carrie Harney of Houston, Texas

Cardstock: **Bazzill Basics** Paper: **7 Gypsies, KI Memories, Rob and Bob Studio** Acrylic letters: **KI Memories** Embroidery floss: **DMC** Chipboard frame: **Heidi Swapp** Rub ons: **Basic Grey** Stickers: **American Crafts**

Cut a strip of dotted paper just shorter than your page and notch one end. Cover a chipboard heart with striped paper; sand the edges before placing it, then hand stitch around the heart and paper with white embroidery floss. Cut a green chipboard frame in half diagonally to create a jumbo photo corner. To customize these green acrylic letters from KI Memories, trace them on white text paper from 7 Gypsies and cut the letters out with an x-acto knife. Adhere them to the back of the acrylic letters using decoupage.

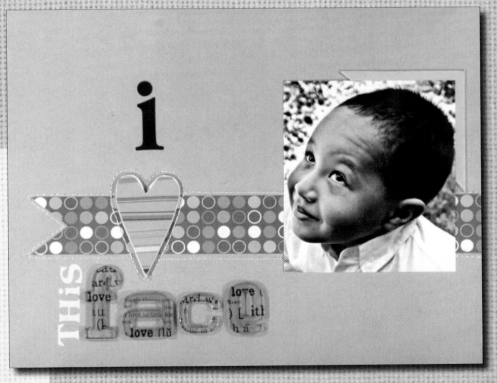

THANK YOU
Paige Taylor

Card is 6 1/4 x 4"
Cardstock: **Bazzill Basics** Paper, acrylic letters: **Heidi Grace** Acrylic token letters: **Doodlebug Design**
Ribbon: **Unknown**

Stagger acrylic letters from Heidi Grace to spell "thank", then use Doodlebug letters to spell "you" below that on a piece of ribbon. Notice how the bright colors stand out against the black background of the card base.

T2SK
Jennifer Gallacher of American Fork, Utah

Cardstock: **Prism** Paper: **Deja Views, Doodlebug Design, KI Memories** Eyelets, jump rings: **Making Memories** Conchos: **Scrapworks** Acrylic letters: **KI Memories** Ribbon: **Craft supply** Die cuts: **Deja Views** Date stamp: **Office supply** Scalloped scissors: **Fiskars** Punches: **EK Success** Font: **Century Gothic**

Cut white textured cardstock about 1/2" smaller than your base orange cardstock and stitch a border around the edge. Cut swirls from smooth white paper and stitch them to the textured cardstock before adding paper, a photo, ribbon and conchos. Use orange acrylic letters for your title, letting them overlap your photo slightly.

BIG SQUEEZE
Rachel Cohara of Brunswick Hills, Ohio

Cardstock: **Unknown** Eyelets: **Making Memories** Ribbon: **Darice, KI Memories, Making Memories, Offray** Circle rub ons: **Fontwerks** Letter rub ons: **KI Memories** Ink: **Archival Ink**

Create a unique photo corner – set two eyelets on adjacent sides of your photo and thread ribbon through; secure ends on the back. Knot multicolored ribbons around the base ribbon and trim the ends short. Apply rows of circle rub ons to the left of your photo, then spell out your title with a mix of acrylic and rub on letters by KI Memories.

SUMMER
Alisha Gordon

Card is 7 x 5"
Paper: **Making Memories** Brads, flowers: **Queen & Co.** Stickers, pen: **American Crafts**

Spell out "summer" on your card base with dark brown letter stickers from American Crafts. Add two trios of Queen & Co. acrylic flowers in opposite corners; keep them in place with colorful brads fastened through their centers.

AVERY

Sarah Klemish of Midland, Michigan

Cardstock: **Bazzill Basics** Paper: **My Mind's Eye**
Brads: **Karen Foster Design** Chipboard, acrylic
silhouette flowers: **Heidi Swapp**

Fill the top portion of an 8 1/2 x 11" page
with two photos and a block of striped
paper. Add two strips of red cardstock
and a chipboard letter & bracket. Arrange
three silhouette flowers by Heidi Swapp
over one of the cardstock strips and fasten
them to the page with aqua brads.

STUBBORN

Doris Sander of Hermitage, Tennessee

Cardstock: **Bazzill Basics** Foliage paper: **Basic
Grey** Dotted paper: **Chatterbox** Acrylic
letters, silk flower: **Heidi Swapp** Paper flower:
Chatterbox Tag: **Avery** Embroidery floss: **DMC**
Buttons, fabric: **Craft supply** Letter stickers:
Li'l Davis Designs Pen: **Zig** Paint: **Folk Art**

Dry brush clear acrylic "ghost
letters" from Heidi Swapp with paint
from the same color family as your
patterned paper. Adhere the letters to
black cardstock for a dramatic effect.
Hand stitch along the edges of both
your paper and photo; glue only three
sides of the photo to the page so you
can slip a journaling tag underneath.

Chipboard

chip·board

(chĭp'bôrd', -bōrd') *n.*

1. *a pasteboard made from discarded paper; a hard material made from wood chips that are pressed together.*
2. *perfect for monograms, tags and more; a fun and versatile scrapbooking embellishment that can be painted, stamped or sanded.*

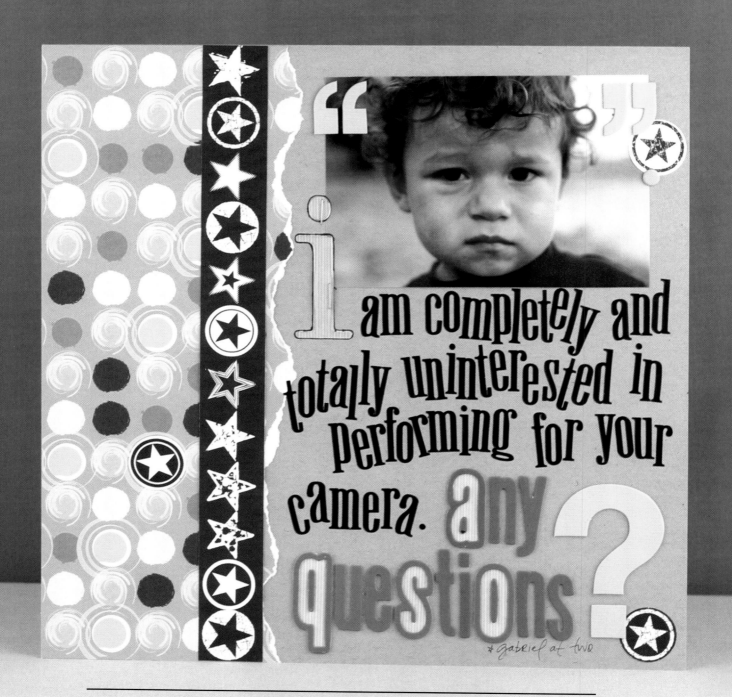

ANY QUESTIONS?

Doris Sander of Hermitage, Tennessee

Cardstock: **Bazzill Basics** Paper: **CherryArte** Brad: **American Crafts** Chipboard letters, letter stickers: **Li'l Davis Designs** Chipboard punctuation, acrylic letter: **Heidi Swapp** Pens: **Sharpie, Zig** Other: **Staples**

A picture is worth a thousand words...especially when your photography subject has a repertoire of facial expressions. Doris translated the look on her son's face into a jumbo title composed of a clear acrylic letter backed by patterned paper, black letter stickers and blue chipboard letters. Doris used the negatives from some of the Li'l Davis letters and backed them with patterned paper before adhering them in place (she used an x-acto knife to trim away the excess). Large chipboard punctuation marks finish the page.

STRIKE A POSE
Christina Padilla of Salinas, California

Cardstock: **Bazzill Basics** Paper: **Basic Grey**
Brads, tags: **Making Memories** Chipboard
letters: **Pressed Petals** Chipboard label holder:
Heidi Swapp Ribbon: **Offray** Flower: **Alexx**
Kesh Ink: **Brilliance** Pen: **Marvy Uchida**

For a title with big impact, stagger green chipboard letters from Pressed Petals atop a pink silk gerbera daisy. Add the subdued remainder of your title with black letter stickers underneath. Draw attention to a Making Memories tag by placing it inside a black chipboard label holder from Heidi Swapp.

LITTLE MARY SUNSHINE
Alissa Fast of Ferndale, Washington

Cardstock, chipboard circles: **Bazzill Basics** Ribbon:
May Arts Stickers, chipboard accents: **Scenic Route**
Paper Co. Ink: **Ranger** Fonts: **2Peas Flower Garden**, from
twopeasinabucket.com, **SP Purkage**, from scrapsupply.com

Sand the edges of these chipboard accents from Scenic Route Paper Co. to create captions for the side of your picture and a colorful photo corner. Incorporate another chipboard piece into your journaling. Alissa covered blank chipboard circles from Bazzill Basics with number stickers for the date and sanded the edges. She also printed flower dingbats in brown ink on patterned paper and cut them out before adhering them over ribbon stems.

I PICK YOU

Lynnise Bowman of Festus, Missouri

Cardstock, brads: **Bazzill Basics** Paper: **Bo-Bunny Press, Daisy D's, Diane's Daughters** Tinker pin: **7 Gypsies** Oval bookplate: **Making Memories** Wire leaf brad: **Karen Foster Design** Ribbon: **Junkitz, unknown** Rustic tags: **Bo-Bunny Press** Die cuts: **Diane's Daughters** Chipboard letters: **Pressed Petals** Rub ons: **Chatterbox** Stickers: **K & Company, Sticko** Newsprint tape: **Club Scrap** Ink: **Cut-it-up.com** Pen: **Zig** Other: **Cork, library pocket**

Sand the edges of these large chipboard letters from Pressed Petals to give them a rustic feel that's in keeping with an autumn-themed layout.

PUMPKIN MUSH
Celeste Smith of West Hartford, Connecticut

Cardstock: **Bazzill Basics** Paper: **American Crafts, Basic Grey, KI Memories, Marcella by Kay, MOD, Scrapworks** Chipboard and acrylic letters, photo corner: **Heidi Swapp** Font: **Rockwell, from myfonts.com**

To the casual observer, it might seem like you are enjoying scooping out that pumpkin. The reality? You really don't like...

PUMPKIN mush

If a key title word happens to be an object in your photo, let them be the same color! Writing "pumpkin" with orange chipboard letters from Heidi Swapp connects the word to the picture and helps bring balance to the page.

FLOWER FOR MAMA
Tara Pakosta of Libertyville, Illinois

Cardstock: **Bazzill Basics** Paper: **Wild Asparagus** Staples: **Making Memories** Acrylic flowers: **Heidi Swapp** Chipboard letters: **We R Memory Keepers** Letter stickers: **American Crafts** Stamps: **Hero Arts** Ink: **StazOn**

Stamp your journaling, letting each word or two have its own scrap of paper. Staple the pieces in place on the bottom half of your layout and add a chipboard and rub on title under the photo. Use these chipboard letters from We R Memory Keepers, choosing one letter that is patterned and letting the rest be solid colors.

FLOWER for Mama

at grams
up north with for you
dandelion wild grass between smiling remembering
in hand abandon the toes when i did
running yelling me waiting this too

hawaiian wedding 2005

love [ləv]
A deep, tender, feeling of affection toward a person, such as that arising from kinship, recognition of attractive qualities, or a sense of underlying oneness.

julie and nathan

so in love

SO IN LOVE
Heather Thompson of Brentwood, California

Paper, chipboard letter, rub ons: **Rusty Pickle** Ink: **Hero Arts** Silver leafing pen: **Krylon** Marker: **Sharpie** Font: **Satisfaction, from myfonts.com** Digital polka-dot ribbon: **Twopeasinabucket.com**

Go over a jumbo chipboard letter from Rusty Pickle with a silver leafing pen. Print a digital polka-dot ribbon and your title on an 8 1/2 x 11" sheet of white cardstock before adding a photo, blocks of patterned paper and the chipboard monogram.

SMIRK
Sarah Klemish of Midland, Michigan

Cardstock: **Bazzill Basics** Paper: **Autumn Leaves** Brads: **American Crafts** Chipboard letters: **Heidi Swapp** Rub ons: **My Mind's Eye** Font: **Bell Gothic**

The I'll tolerate you taking "one" more picture but I won't like it

Notice how Sarah has used circles to great effect: the photo is a semi-circle, the patterned paper has circles and colored brads border the paper. To top it off, a large orange circle backs one of the chipboard title letters, giving the whole layout a cohesive feel. The uneven circles on the paper and the wavy stitching rub ons from My Mind's Eye help keep the circle motif from feeling too uniform.

TYBEE ISLAND
Becky Thackston of Hiram, Georgia

Paper: **Basic Grey** Ribbon charm, twill: **Stampin' Up!** Chipboard letters: **Heidi Swapp** Ric rac: **Craft supply** Ink: **Tim Holtz** Black pen: **Pigma Micron** White gel pen: **Uniball Signo**

If you've got beach pictures, leave your chipboard letters unpainted, unsanded and otherwise unadorned for a dimensional title that stands out but still coordinates with the sand and sea.

Tybee Island
Savannah, Georgia Spring 2004

YOU
Heather Keller of Humble, Texas

Cardstock, ribbon: **Bazzill Basics** Paper: **Chatterbox** Heart charm: **Craft supply** Ribbon slide: **Maya Road** Chipboard letters and bracket: **Basic Grey** Acrylic tokens: **KI Memories** Twill: **Carolee's Creations, Creative Impressions** Flowers: **Heidi Swapp** Fabric tab: **Scrapworks** Ink: **Stampin' Up!** Paint: **Making Memories**

Create an eye-catching title with jumbo chipboard letters from Basic Grey. Cover one with patterned paper and paint the rest. Once dry, ink the edges of all the letters brown. Add interest by tying a ribbon and charm around one letter.

CUTE BABY SMILING

Shelby Valadez of Saugus, CA

Tan cardstock: **Bazzill Basics** Paper: **Scenic Route Paper Co.** Chipboard letter: **Basic Grey** Ink: **Stampin' Up!** Corner rounder: **Marvy Uchida** Font: **2Peas Tubby**, from twopeasinabucket.com

Place a large chipboard letter from Basic Grey on vertical striped paper, trace around it and cut out. Adhere the paper to the chipboard and ink the edges. When arranging the elements on your page, set the chipboard letter over horizontally striped paper for contrast.

absolutely
nothing better than a
cute baby smiling
thomas 6/05

GREAT CHEESE...

Summer Fullerton of Tigard, Oregon

Cardstock: **Bazzill Basics** Paper: **Chloe's Closet, Fancy Pants Designs, Foof-a-La** Ribbon: **Foof-a-La,** unknown Thread: **Making Memories** Chipboard letters: **Heidi Swapp** Wood frame: **Fancy Pants Designs** Buttons: **Foof-a-La, SEI** Rub ons: **Gin-X, Making Memories** Stickers: **Arctic Frog** Photo corner punch: **EK Success** Ink: **ColorBox** Paint: **Plaid** Label maker: **Dymo** Other: **Crystal lacquer, chipboard**

Summer cut photo corners from chipboard, covered them with Foof-a-La patterned paper and applied a layer of crystal lacquer to finish. She then used them as arrows to draw the eye to her focal photo. The hidden journaling on the tag tells the story of taking a road trip up the Oregon coast with her husband and stopping at the Tillamook Cheese factory on the way.

GREAT CHEESE comes from HAPPY COWS

HAPPY COWS COME FROM

OREGON

Tillamook Cheese

PULL

Die Cuts

die cut

(dĭ kŭt) *n.*

1. *an engraved metal piece for impressing a design.*
2. *in scrapbooking, a wide variety of alphabets, tags, titles and more that are used to embellish layouts and cards.*

POCKET FULL OF POSIES
Tisha McCuiston of Midlothian, Virginia

Cardstock: **Bazzill Basics** Paper, buttons, rub ons: **SEI** Square punch: **Marvy Uchida**

Punch nine squares from coordinating SEI paper; arrange them in a large "L" across the bottom and up the left side. Place your photo in the middle of the page and apply a rub on title and rub on stitches. Three trios of buttons complete the look.

YOUR TURN
Kelly Goree of Shelbyville, Kentucky

Cardstock: **Bazzill Basics** Paper: **KI Memories, Pebbles, Inc.** Conchos, die cuts: **Scrapworks** Chipboard letters: **Making Memories** Stickers: **Chatterbox** Paint: **Plaid** Font: **Century Gothic**

Break up the line where photo meets paper with two circle die cuts held in place with coordinating conchos. Place two more in the bottom right corner next to your journaling to continue the circle motif.

SUNSHINE DAYDREAM
Peg Manrique of Sunderland, Vermont

Cardstock: **Bazzill Basics** Paper: **K & Company** Die cut: **Deluxe Cuts** Rub ons: **Scrapworks** Vellum letter: **Memories Complete** Other: **Jumbo paperclip**

Frame the first letter of your child's name with a colorful sun die cut that stands out against the patterned background. Spell out your title with blue letter rub ons.

{ reason you're such a great friend #497:

we have fun together even when we're just

chillin'

out →

CHILLIN'
Tammy Morrill

Card is 4 1/4 x 6 1/4"
Blue cardstock: **Bazzill Basics** Patterned cardstock: **Chatterbox** Orange paper: **Art Warehouse**
Brads and tag: **Making Memories** Bracket stamp: **Green Grass Stamps** Ink: **Close To My Heart**
Pen: **Staedtler**

Incorporate a tag into your sentiment by writing above and below it on your card front.

BACKYARD BALL

Jennifer Gallacher of American Fork, Utah

Cardstock: **Prism** Paper: **Deja Views, Sandylion** Brads, embroidery floss: **Making Memories** Blue and red paper clips, ribbon, stitched border, chipboard letters, label stickers: **Li'l Davis Designs** Silver paper clips: **Office supply** Acrylic token: **KI Memories** Border die cut, rub ons: **Deja Views** Tag stickers: **Doodlebug Design** Circle punch: **EK Success** Font: **Antique Type**, from scrapvillage.com

Jennifer used a circle cutter to cut the baseball from white cardstock. She outlined the edge with black pen, then traced two curves with a pencil, stitched red thread to the ball and added Doodlebug tag stickers along the bottom. A 1" circle punch from McGill is just the right size to back a KI Memories acrylic token, placed at the top of Jennifer's secondary photo. The strip of red paper between the journaling strip and the base green cardstock helps the chipboard title letters stand out.

LEAVING LAS VEGAS

Kelly Purkey of Chicago, Illinois

Cardstock: **Bazzill Basics** Paper, brads, pen: **American Crafts** Die cuts: **KI Memories** Stickers: **American Crafts, office supply** Rub ons: **7 Gypsies**

Mat large die cut letters from KI Memories on white cardstock, trim out and ink the edges. Space "leaving" letter stickers across the left side of your layout, setting a colored brad between each letter. Keep your "Las Vegas" die cuts left-justified, then add two matted photos. For an original journaling block, overlap and stagger office supply label stickers.

HI
Tina Gonzales

Card is 6" square
Cardstock: **Bazzill Basics** Paper: **American Crafts** Chipboard letters: **Pressed Petals**

Make a tri-fold card from double-sided American Crafts paper; adhere patterned paper to the solid side, leaving a 1/4" border. Jumbo chipboard letters from Pressed Petals make a big statement that stands out.

I LOVE YOU
Sybille Moen of Tarzana, California

Cardstock: **Bazzill Basics** Brads: **Heidi Swapp** Acrylic tokens, die cuts: **KI Memories** Flowers: **Prima**

Begin by placing a photo on blue cardstock, centered toward the bottom left. Use an eyelet setter to punch holes in the outline of a heart (pencil it in first if you'd like). Mat the piece on a slightly larger piece of dark pink cardstock and stitch a large heart around the hole-punched outline. Double stitch around the border. Put a sheet of die cuts from KI Memories to good use and arrange die cut quotes in a collage on one side of the heart; add flowers and acrylic tokens. Spell out the rest of your sentiment with large die cut letters.

FUN IN THE SUN
Monica Schoenemann
of Flower Mound, Texas

Cardstock: **Bazzill Basics** Brads, stickers: **American Crafts** Photo turns: **7 Gypsies** Ribbon: **American Crafts, Michaels** Die cut arrows and photo corners: **QuicKutz** Rub ons: **Basic Grey** Font: **Tahoma**

Draw attention to the funny faces in your photos with these arrow die cuts from QuicKutz; die cut photo corners in the same color. Knot ribbon to photo turns and adhere between strips of printed journaling to create flower petals; a large rub on from Basic Grey makes the flower.

FRESH
Alisha Gordon

Card is 4 1/2 x 5"
Cardstock: **Bazzill Basics, Die Cuts with a View** Ribbon: **American Crafts, Scrapworks** Flowers: **Jolee's Boutique** Tag: **Making Memories**

Stitch a block of green cardstock to a purple card base; round the corners. Adhere three folded pieces of purple ribbon to the inside of the card. Add a large tag from Making Memories and small Jolee's Boutique flower stickers.

SWOON

Staci Etheridge of McKinney, Texas

Cardstock: **Bazzill Basics** Paper: **Anna Griffin, Colorbök** Letter stickers: **American Crafts** Heart stickers: **Pebbles, Inc.** Ink: **ColorBox** White gel pen: **Uniball Signo**

Let one dramatic black & white photo take center stage by placing it on black cardstock with an avalanche of hearts spilling out from underneath. Half a heart, cut from patterned paper, creates the base, while heart stickers overlap each other in a jumble of red, pink and green. Staci spelled "swoon" with black letter stickers on black cardstock, then traced around them with a white gel pen.

SUMMERTIME BOY

Heather Thompson of Brentwood, California

Cardstock: **Bazzill Basics** Paper: **Chatterbox, KI Memories** Tags: **KI Memories, Making Memories** Ribbon: **Offray, fabric supply** Buttons: **Blumenthal Lansing Co.** Stickers: **Creative Imaginations, Pebbles, Inc.** Rub ons: **SEI** Ink: **Hero Arts** Pen: **American Crafts**

Ink the edges of quotes cut from KI Memories patterned paper and arrange them in a collage next to your photo.

Retail Store Directory

ONLINE STORE DIRECTORY

ALLY SCRAPS
www.allyscraps.com

BLESSINGS RECEIVED
www.stores.ebay.com/blessings-received

EXPRESSIVE SCRAPBOOKS
www.expressivescrapbooks.com

OBG'S UNDERGROUND SCRAPBOOKING SUPPLY CO.
COEURD' ALENE, ID
208-664-6010
orginalsbygina@hotmail.com
www.obgunderground.com

THE SCRAP STOP
www.thescrapstop.com

URBAN SCRAPPER
www.urbanscrapperonline.com

ARIZONA

BINDING MEMORIES BY IDA
1150 DUCE OF CLUBS STE C
SHOWLOW, AZ 85901
(928) 537-8116

CALIFORNIA

PAGES IN TYME
560 PINE KNOTT BLVD STE B
BIG BEAR LAKE, CA 92315
909-866-3661
M-S 10-6 SUN 10-5

SCRAPBOOK BLESSINGS
1560 NEWBURY ROAD STE 5
NEWBURY PARK, CA 91320
805-375-1568
M-Sat 9-6
service@scrapbookblessings.com
www.scrapbookblessings.com

SCRAPBOOK NOOK
444 SAN MATEO AVE.
SANBRUNO, CA 94066
650-588-3112

SCRAPBOOK OASIS
17895 SKY PARK CIRCLE SUITE H
IRVINE, CA 92614
949-756-2729
www.thescrapbookoasis.typepad.com

STAMPERS WAREHOUSE
101-G TOWN & COUNTRY DR
DANVILLE, CA 94526
(925) 362-9595
www.stamperswarehouse.com

TABLE SCRAPZ
1002 BREA MALL
BREA, CA 92821
(714) 529-6887
m-f 10-9 sat 10-7 sun 11-6

COLORADO

THE TREASURE BOX
1833 E. HARMONY RD #1
FORT COLLINS, CO 80528
970-207-9939
M-F 9:30-6 TH 9:30-9
SAT 10-5

CONNECTICUT

NEW ENGLAND SCRAPBOOK CO
200 ALBANY TURNPIKE-RTE 44
CANTON, CT 06019
860-693-9197
M-tu 10-6 W-th 10-9 F-sat 10-10
Sun 12-6
www.newenglandscrapbook.com

DELAWARE

HEARTFELT MEMORIES
110 B ASTRO SHOPPING CENTER
KIRKWOOD HIGHWAY
NEWARK, DE 19711
(302) 369-9301
m-w 10-6 th-sat 9-5 fri 9-11
www.heartfelt-memories.com

FLORIDA

CROPPIN' CORNER
175-C NE EGLIN PKWY
FT.WALTON BEACH, FL 32548
850-581-2767
M ,W-F 9-6 TUE 9-8 SAT 9-5
www.croppincornerfl.com

SCRAPBOOK CROSSING
4761 N. CONGRESS AVE.
BOYNTON, FL. 33426
561-439-8700
www.scrapbookcrossing.net
scrapcrossing@aol.com

TIFFY NEW YORK
15421 W DIXIE HWY BAY 9
NORTH MIAMI BEACH FL. 33162
305-582-3731/305-944-3332
tiffyny@aol.com
www.tiffynewyork.com

GEORGIA

SCRAPBOOK OUTLET
PRIME OUTLET S-CALHOUN #90
CALHOUN, GA 30701
706-602-3555
I-75, EXIT 312, 40 ML N OF ATLANTA
Scrapbookoutlet.com

HAWAII

THE SCRAPPERS' DEN
719 KAMEHANEHER HWY SUITE C201
PEARL CITY, HI 96782
808-455-4100
T-FR 10-6, SAT 10-4 SUN 11-3
www.scrappersden.com

IDAHO

A SCRAPPERS & STAMPERS DELIGHT
TIFFANY SQUARE
156 MAIN AVE N.
TWIN FALLS, ID 83301
208-736-7286
mary@scrapthatsmile.com
www.scrapthatsmile.com

CINDY'S
34 NORTH MAIN ST
MALAD, ID 83252
208-766-2666
www.cindysscrapbooking.com

ILLINOIS

SCRAP N STAMP ART
901 SOUTH NEIL ST, STE B
CHAMPAIGN, IL 61820
217-352-0532
M-F 10-6, SAT 10-5, SUN 11-5
www.scrapnstampart.com

INDIANA

SCHMITT PHOTO
4847 PLAZA EAST BLVD
EVANSVILLE, IN 47715
812-473-0245
M-F 8:30-8 SAT 9-6 SUN 1-5
www.schmittphoto.com

SCRAPBOOK OUTLET
PRIME OUTLET- FREMONT #10
FREMONT, IN 46737
260-833-2767
I-69 AND 80/90 TOLL ROAD
Scrapbookoutlet.com

SCRAPBOOK XANADU
5459 E. 82ND ST
IDIANAPOLIS, IN 46250
317-579-2500
M-F 10-9 SAT 10-7 SUN 12-5
www.scrapbookxanadu.com

SCRAPBOOK XANADU
520 N. STATE RD #135
GREENWOOD, IN 46142
317-885-7200
M-F 10-9 SAT 10-7 SUN 12-5
www.scrapbookxanadu.com

KENTUCKY

SCRAPBOOK OUTLET
DRY RIDGE OUTLET CENTER #1106
DY RIDGE, KY 41035
859-823-2767
I-75 25 ML S. OF CINCINNATI
Scrapbookoutlet.com

MAINE

MEMORY LANE
20 COBURN ST
AUBURN, ME 04210
207-782-1600
memorylanepages@aol.com
www.memorylanepages.com

THE MEMORYBOOK WORKSHOP
THE GRAY PLAZA
GRAY MAIN, ME 04039
207-657-4566
cindy@memorybookworkshop.com
www.memorybookworkshop.com

MASSACHUSETTS

LEAVE A LEGACY SCRAPBOOKING
1510 NEW STATE HWY RT 44 UNIT 18
RAYNHAM, MA 02767
508-880-6900
M-CLOSED, T-TH 10-8,
W,F,SAT 10-6 SUN 12-4
www.leavealegacyscrapbooking .com

MICHIGAN

PAGES IN TIME
6323 C WEST SAGINAW HWY
LANSING, MI 48917
517-327-5526

MINNESOTA

MEMORY BOX
38 N. UNION ST.
MORA, MN 55051
320-679-3439
www.memorybox.biz

MISSOURI

THE SCRAP OUTLET.COM
1320 W 40 HWY
ODESSA, MO 64076
816-230-5579
LOCATED AT THE ODESSA OUTLET MALL
www.thescrapoutlet.com
COME VISIT OUR WEB SITE FOR
FREE OFFERS

NEW YORK

YOUR HAPPY PLACE
272 LARKFIELD RD
E. NORTHPORT, NY 11731
www.yourhappyplaceonline.com

NORTH CAROLINA

A PAGE IN TIME
1216-A PARKWAY DR.
GOLDSBORO, NC 27534
919-344-7884
Arlene@apgntime.com
www.apgntime.com

ENCHANTED COTTAGE
RUBBER STAMP & SCRAPBOOKS
JUST WEST OF WINSTON-SALEM
6275 SHALLOWFORD RD
LEWISVILLE, NC 27023
336-945-5889
M 10-3 T, W, F 10-5:30 TH 10-8 SAT 10-4
www.enchantedcottagenc.com

OHIO

COUNTRY CROSSING
& CROPPERS CORNER
IN FRONT OF WALMART
CORNER OF STATE RT 250
&WESTWIND DR
NORWALK,OH 44857
419-663-0496
postmaster@cropperscorner.net
www.cropperscorner.net

CROP-PAPER-SCISSORS, INC.
3583 MEDINA ROAD
MEDINA, OH 44256
330-723-6171
M 10-5 T-F 10-8 SAT 10-6 SUN 1-5
www.crop-paper-scissors.com

SCRAPBOOK OUTLET
PRIME OUTLETS- LODI #175
BURBANK, OHIO 44214
330-948-8080
I-71, EXIT 204, 20 ML S OF
CLEVELAND
Scrapbookoutlet.com

OKLAHOMA

SCRAPBOOKS!
12325 N. MAY AVE STE 105
OKLAHOMA CITY, OK 73120
405-749-2266
www.scrapbooks!.com

SCRAPBOOKS FROM THE HEART
11649 S. WESTERN AVE.
OKLAHOMA CITY, OK 73170
405-692-6491
M-S 10-6, SUN 1-5
www.scrapbooksfromtheheartokc.com

SCRAP HAPPYS
7142 S. MEMORIAL DR.
TULSA, OK 74133
918-250-0472
M-W, S 10-6 TH-F 10-8 SUN 1-5
www.scraphappys.com

OREGON

SCATTERED PICTURES
13852 NE SANDY BLVD
PORTLAND, OR 97230
503-252-1888
TU, TH,F- 10-5 W 10-8 SAT 10-4
CLOSED MON & SUN

SCRAP-A-DOODLE
354 NE NORTON SUITE 200
BEND, OR 97701
541-388-0311
scrapyard@empnet.com
www.scrap-a-doodle.com

SCRAP Happens! Inc.
1250 LANCASTER DR S.E.
SALEM, OR 97301
503-566-8870
M-TH, 10-8 F10-11 PM SAT 10-6 SUN 1-5
www.scraphappens.net

PENNSYLVANIA

SCRAPBOOK SUPER STATION
A CRAFTERS HOME STORE
168 POINT PLAZA
BUTLER, PA 16001
724-287-4311
SUN 12-5 MON-SAT 10-9
www.scrapbookstation.com

TENNESSEE

THE CROP SHOP
7616 LEE HWY BLDG B
CHATTANOOGA, TN 37421
423-899-3515
store@cropshoponline.com
www.cropshoponline.com

TEXAS

JUST 4 FUN SCRAPBOOKING
2540 E. BROADWAY STE C
PEARLAND, TX 77581
261-412-7338

LONE STAR
SCRAPBOOK COMPANY
27842 1-45 N.
THE WOOD LANDS, TX 77385
281-296-2296
sales@lonestarscrapbook.com
www.lonestarscrapbook.com

NOVEL APPROACH
607 S FRIENDSWOOD DR. #15
FRIENDSWOOD, TX 77546
281-992-3137
www.booksandscraps.com

PAULA PICKLES SCRAPBOOKS
STE 39 E1 MERCADO MALL
712 N.77 SUNSHINE STRIP
HARLINGEN, TX 78550
956-440-1222
picklescraps@sbcglobal.net
www.paulapickles.com

SCRAPBOOK VILLAGE
3424 FM 1092 STE 270
MISSOURI CITY, TX 77459
281-208-5251
www.thescrapbookvillage.com

SCRAP STOP
3750 GATTIS SCHOOL ROAD STE 500
ROUND ROCK, TX 78664
512-246-9070
M-SAT 9-9 SUN 12-6
www.scrapstop.com

UTAH

SCRAPPILY EVERAFTER
996 N. MAIN STREET
TOOELE, UT 84074
435-843-7741
M 10-6, TUE-SAT 10-7
scrappily@hotmail.com

VERMONT

CREATIONS ABOUND
1 CHAMPLAIN COMMONS
ST ALBANS, VT 05478
TOLL FREE 877-517-3521
info@creationsabound.com
www.creationsabound.com

VIRGINIA

ALL ABOUT SCRAPBOOK
2137 UPTON DRIVE, STE 328
VIRGINIA BEACH, VA 23454
(RED MILLS COMMONS)
757-563-9009
www.allaboutscrapbooksonline.com

WASHINGTON

A LITTLE BIT OF HEAVEN
7912 MARTIN WAY E
OLYMPIA, WA 98516
360-493-1707
OPEN 7 DAYS A WEEK,
M-SAT 10-8, SUN 11-5
www.alittlebitofheavenscrapbooking.com

SCRAPBOOKER'S DELIGHT
1160 YEA AVE
BLAINE, WA 98230
604-536-55557

WISCONSIN

THE SCRAPBOOK STORE 3
5042 S. 74TH ST.
GREENFIELD, WI 53220
262-255-2521
www.scrapbook-store.com

CANADA

MAKING MEMORIES
WITH SCRAPBOOKING
4415 HASTING ST
BURNABY, BC V5C 2K1
604-299-3601
makingmemories@telus.net
www.makingmemorieswithscrapbooking.com

SCRAPBOOKER'S DELIGHT
102-14936-32 AVE.
SURREY BC CANADA V4P 3R6
604-536-5557
www.scrapbookersdelight.net

Advertising Directory

Summer 's here and the surf's up! North Shore bodaciously complements all things summer, bright and fun. Coordinating cardstock, stickers, chipboard and rub-ons will make any scrapbooking project a perfect 10! Ask for the North Shore Collection by Scenic Route Paper Co. at your favorite scrapbook shack.

www.scenicroutepaper.com

Scenic Route Paper Co.

It's in the Bag!

Indulge your creativity with the 2006 Colour Collection. Designed to have the look of your favorite cosmetic line, this amazing collection is packed with products to make your scrapbook shine.

858.613-7858   •   www.QueenandCompany.com

QUEEN & Co.

I'D RATHER BE SCRAPPING

CELEBRATE SUMMER!

Will 'n Way™
clear creative ideas

4x8 Boys Toys

4x8 Mz Wee Wee

4x8 Campin' Bear

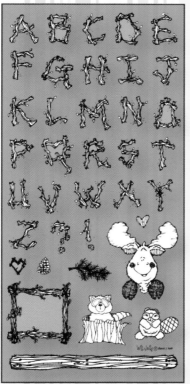

4x8 Moose Sticks

4x8 Stars 'n Stripes

Our best 'summer hint':
Take a Will 'n Way
clear stamp set on
YOUR vacation!
Clear stamps are easy
to pack and organize
and most of all..easier
to STAMP with!
Visit our website and
see the entire
Will 'n Way clear
stamp line...and we'll
give YOU a 'clear'
reason to SMILE this
Summer!

www.djinkers.com

Available at
fine craft
stores near
YOU!

Babies

BabyFace

Sweet face. Girlie face. Chubby face.
Smiling face. Angelic face. Happy face.
Jorianna's face. {05/05}

cute as a bug